The most tender and romantic Coloring book and Doodle Book for adults

Madame Helene art

If you love to create beautiful pictures, then this book is for you. The book contains the most romantic and delicate patterns to fill color. Fill the color of life, use a pencil, pen or ink. All a bit of time and you have a real masterpiece. Draw, zanimayies creativity, fill your soul with beauty and harmony.

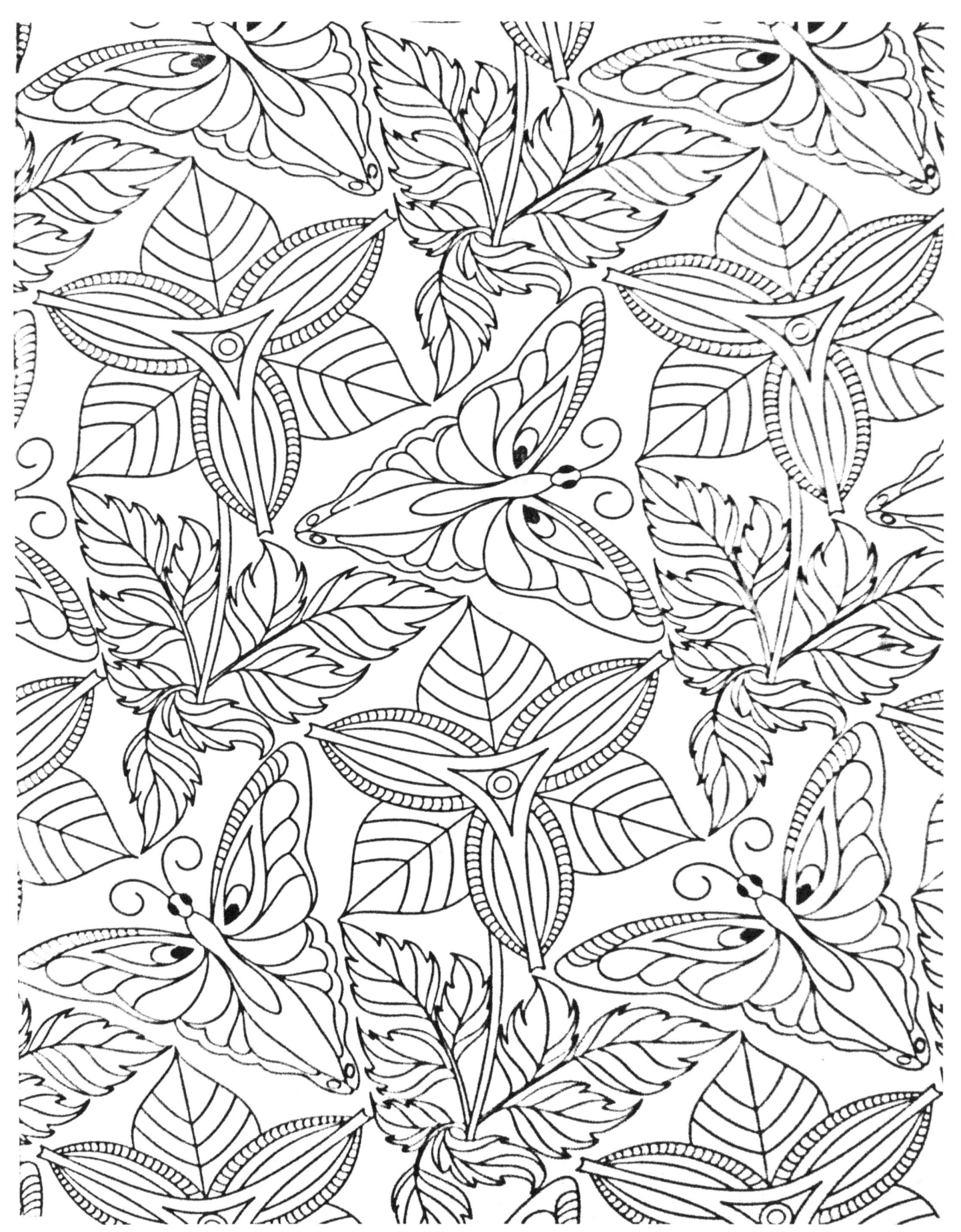

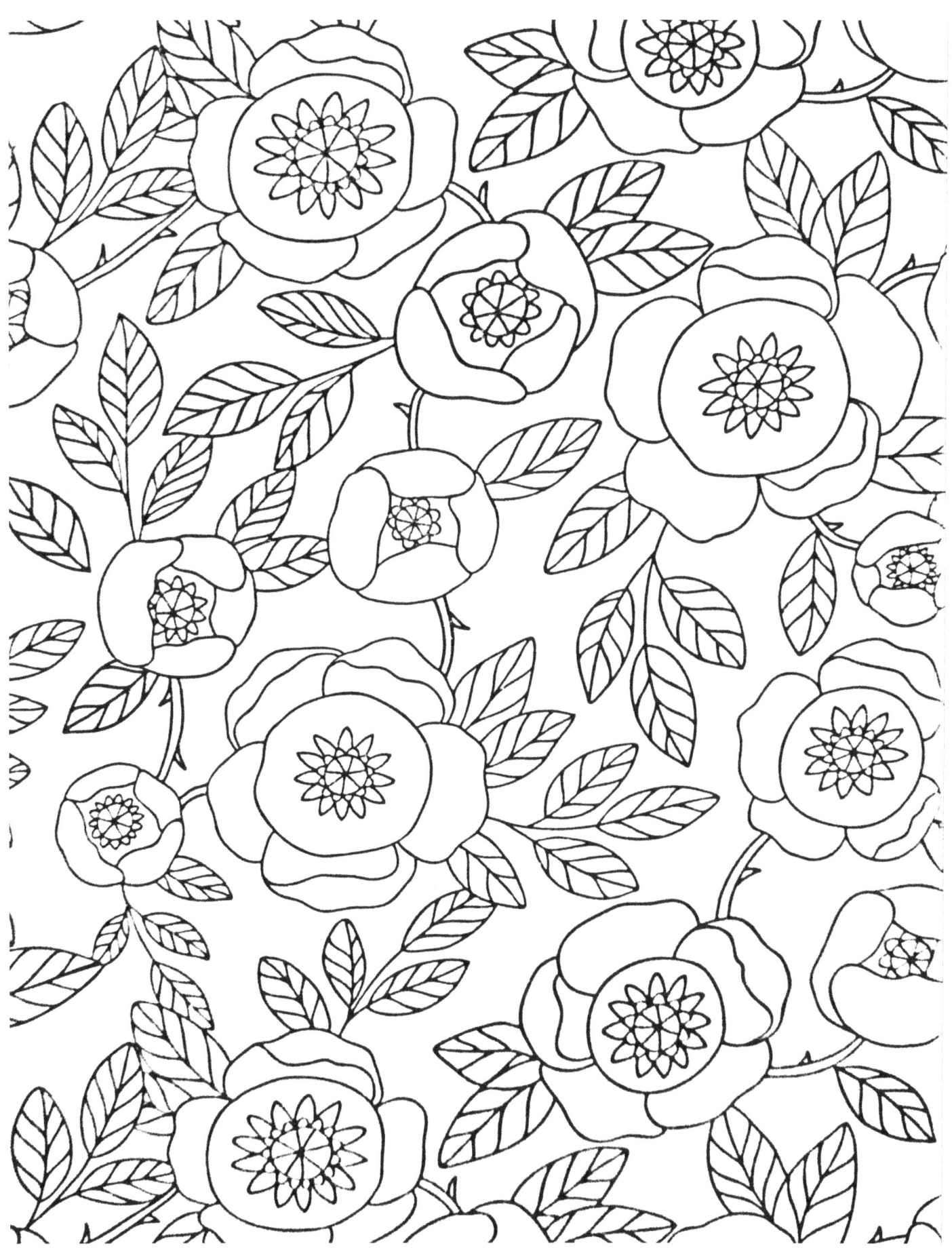

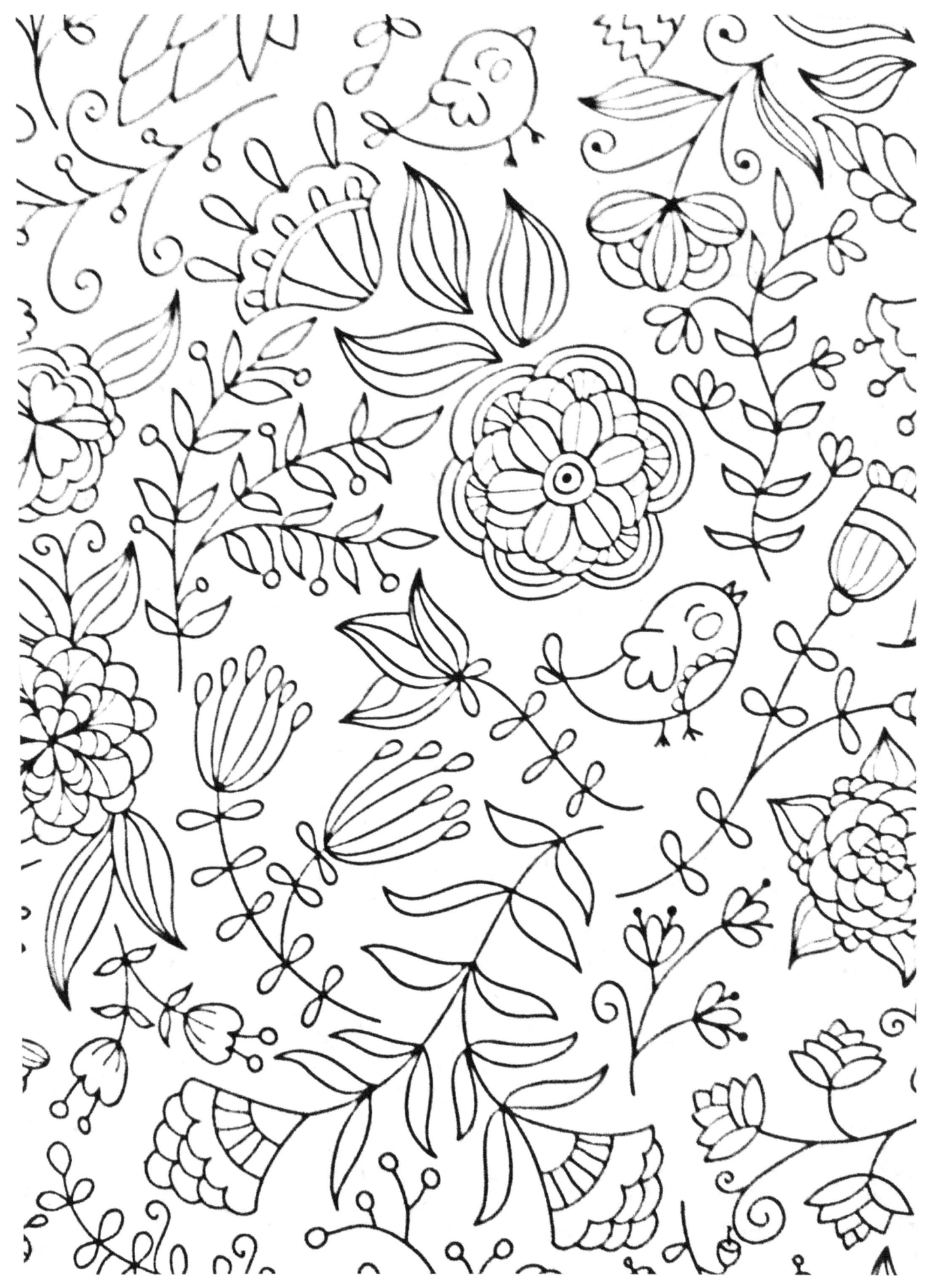

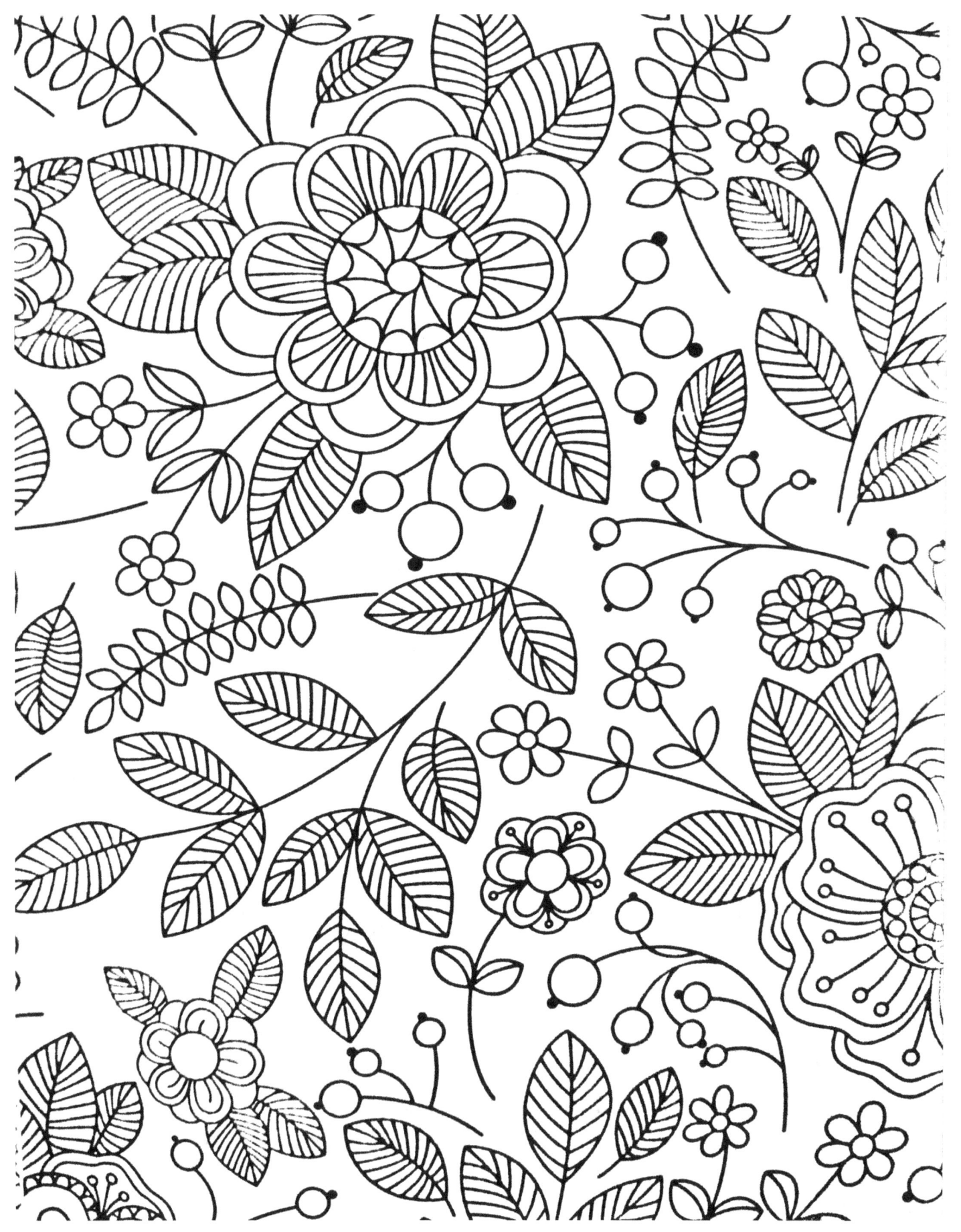

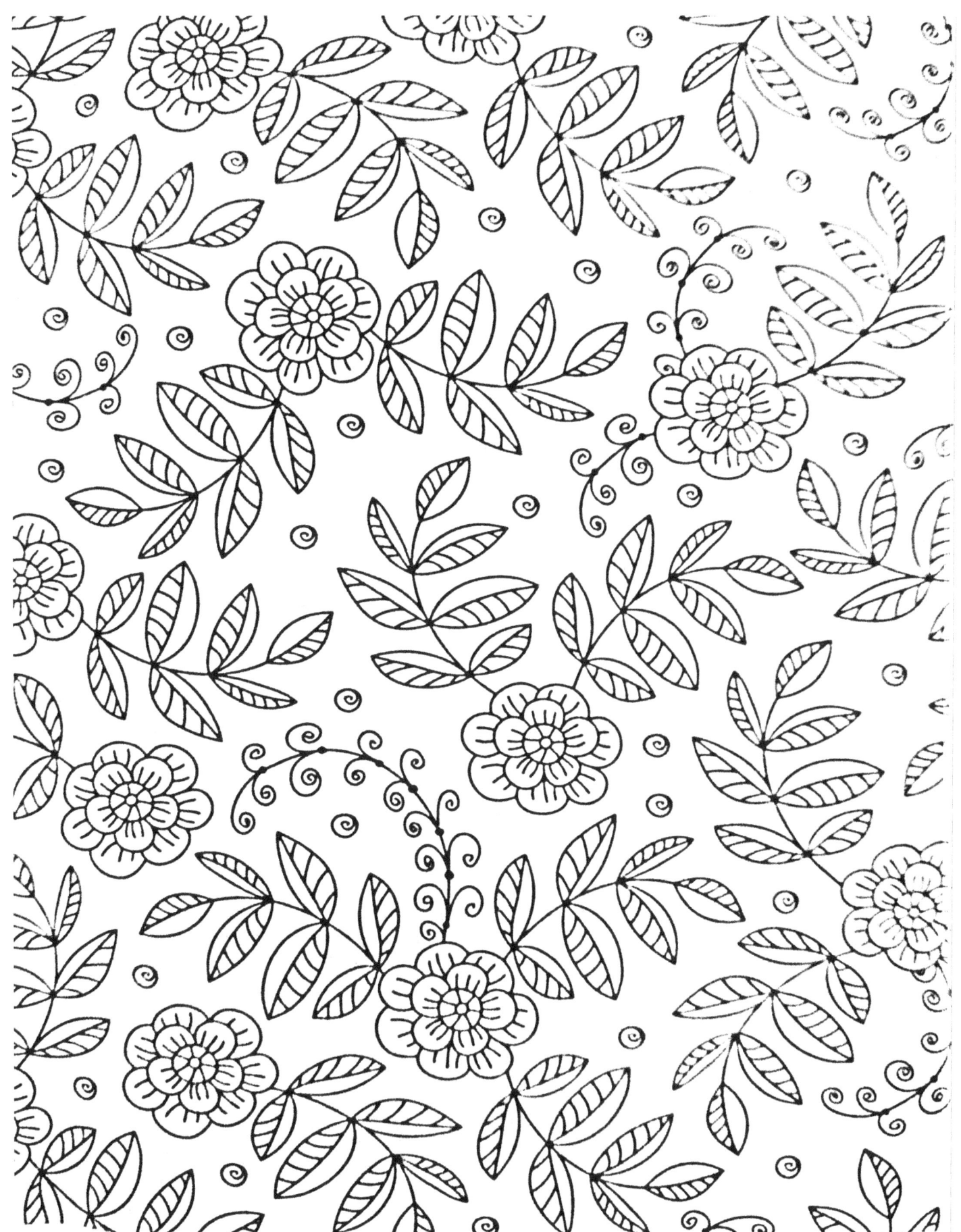

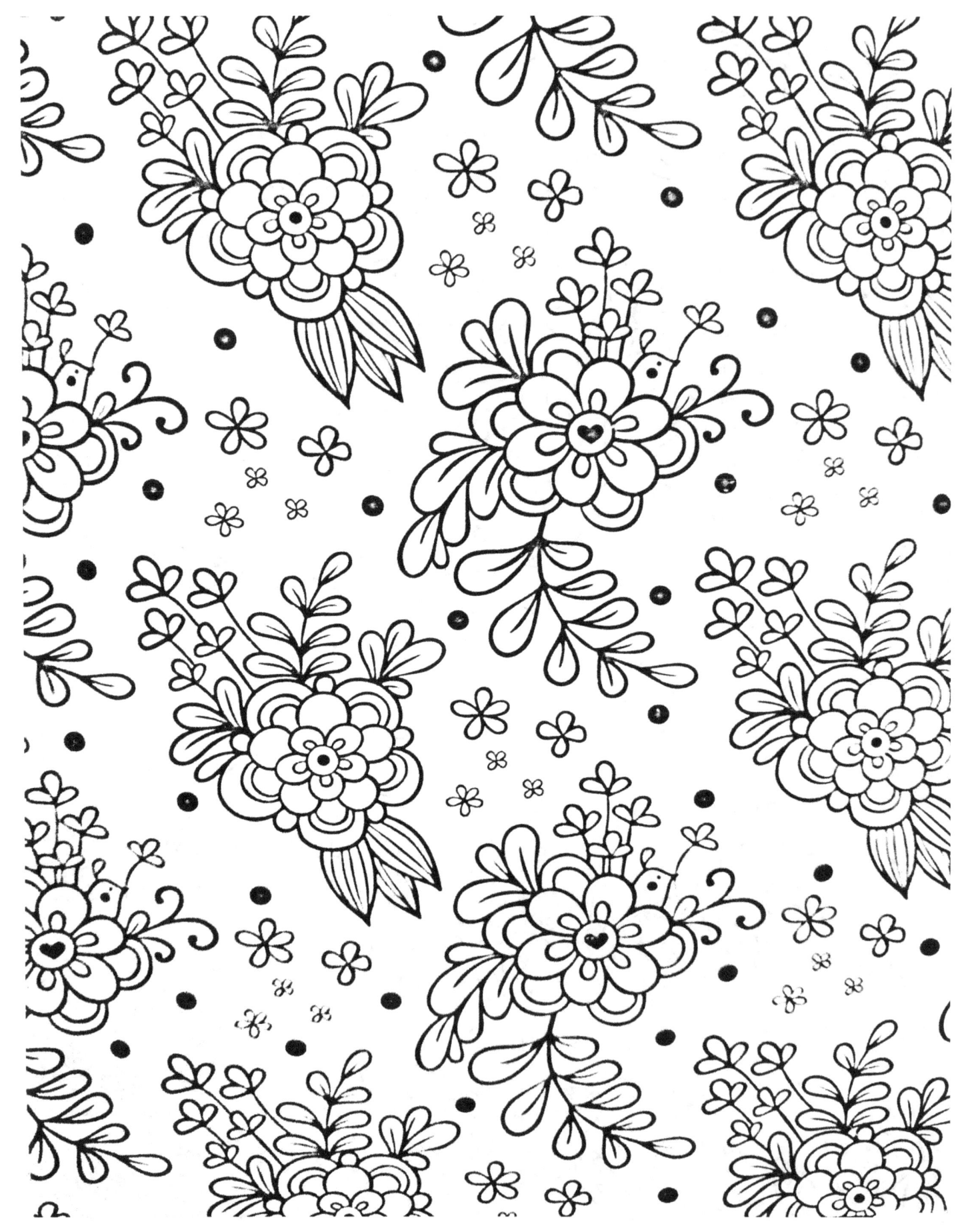

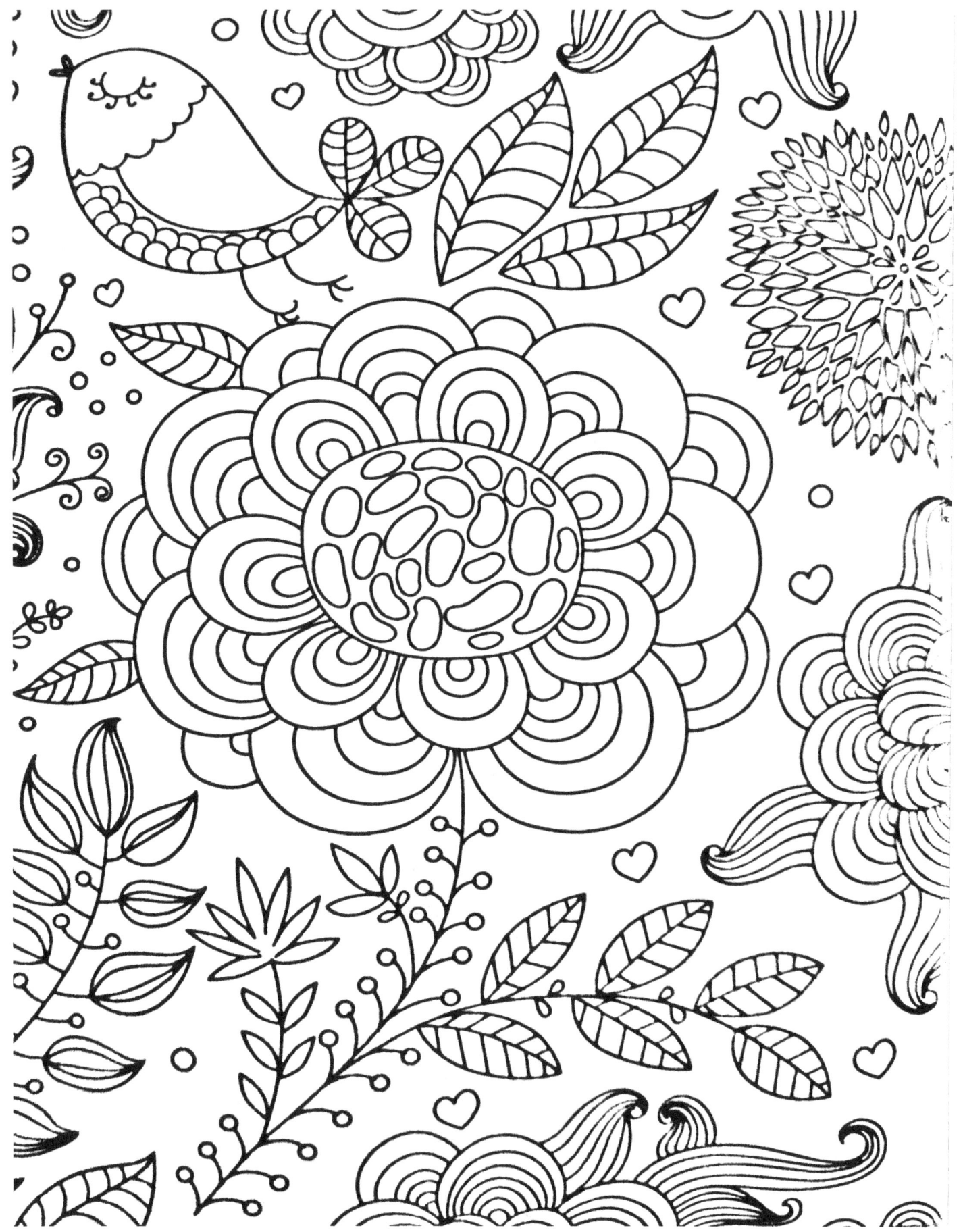

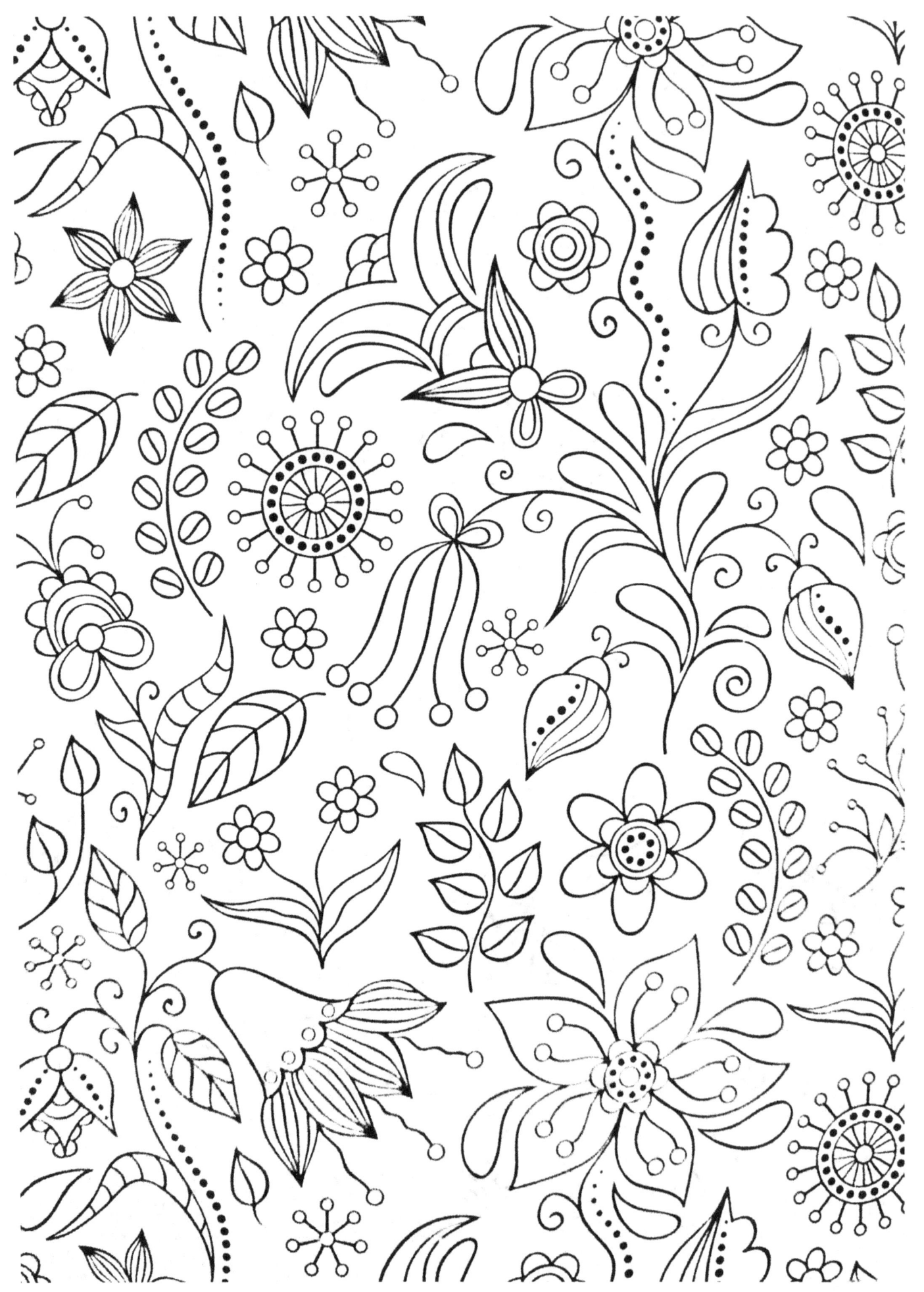

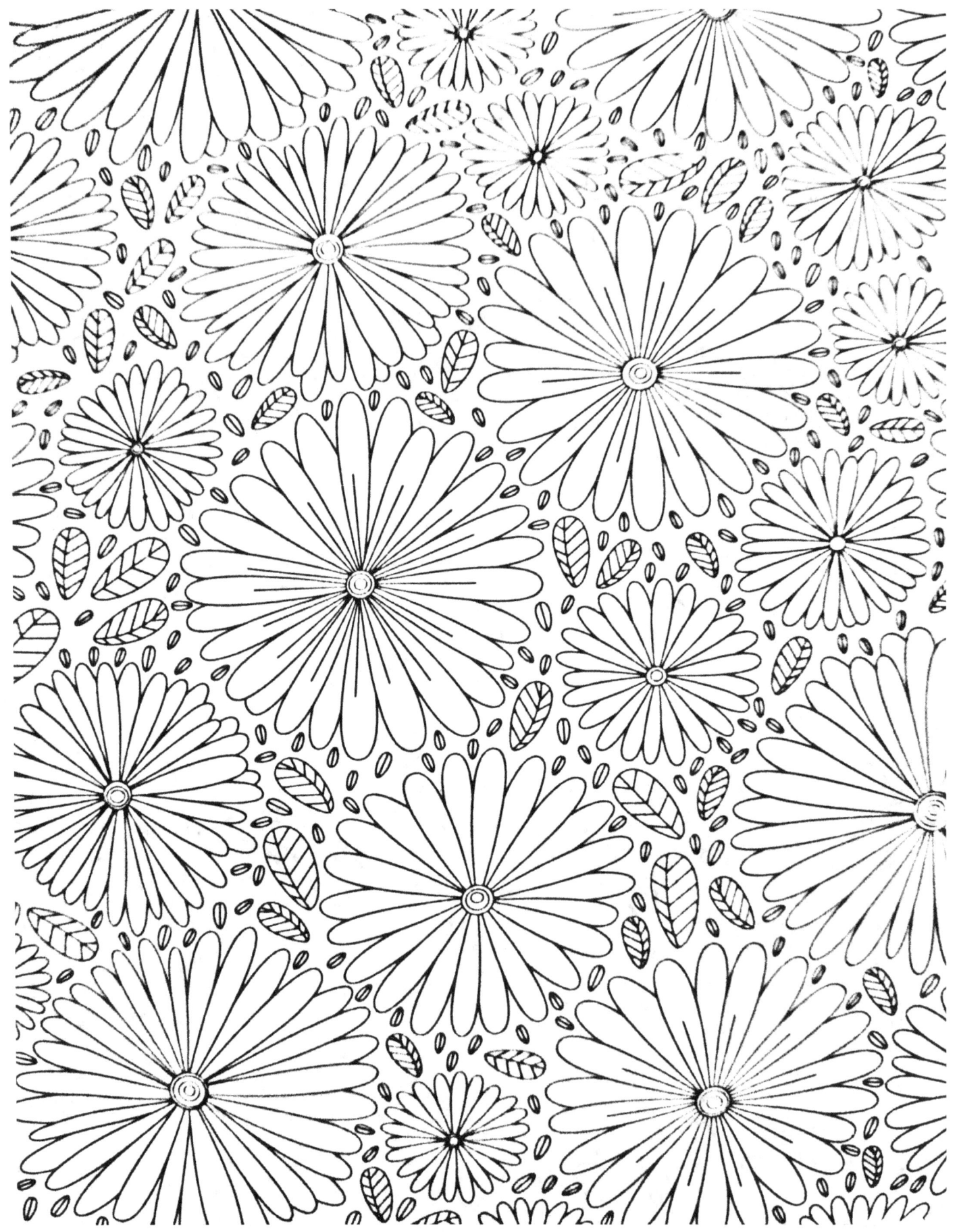

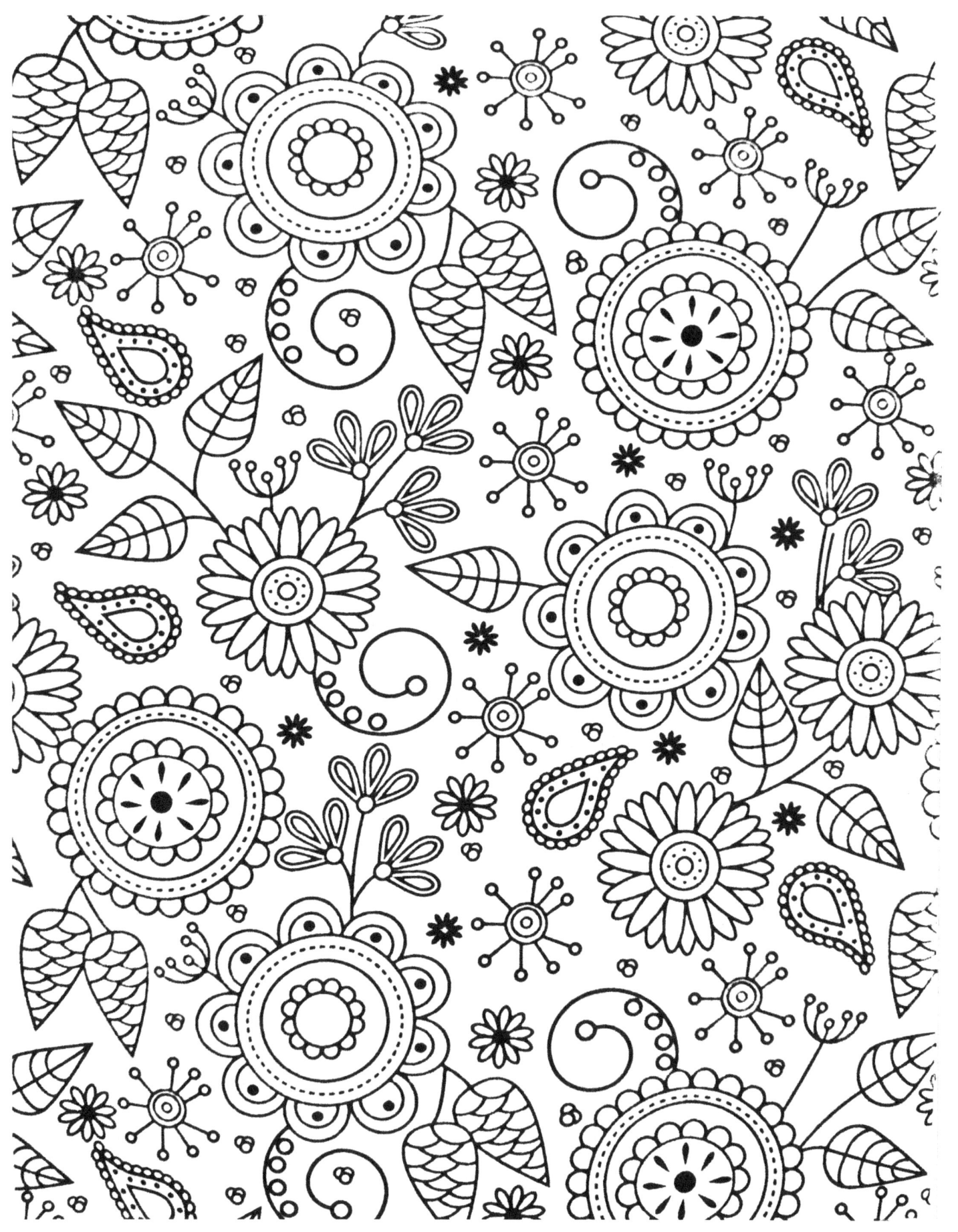

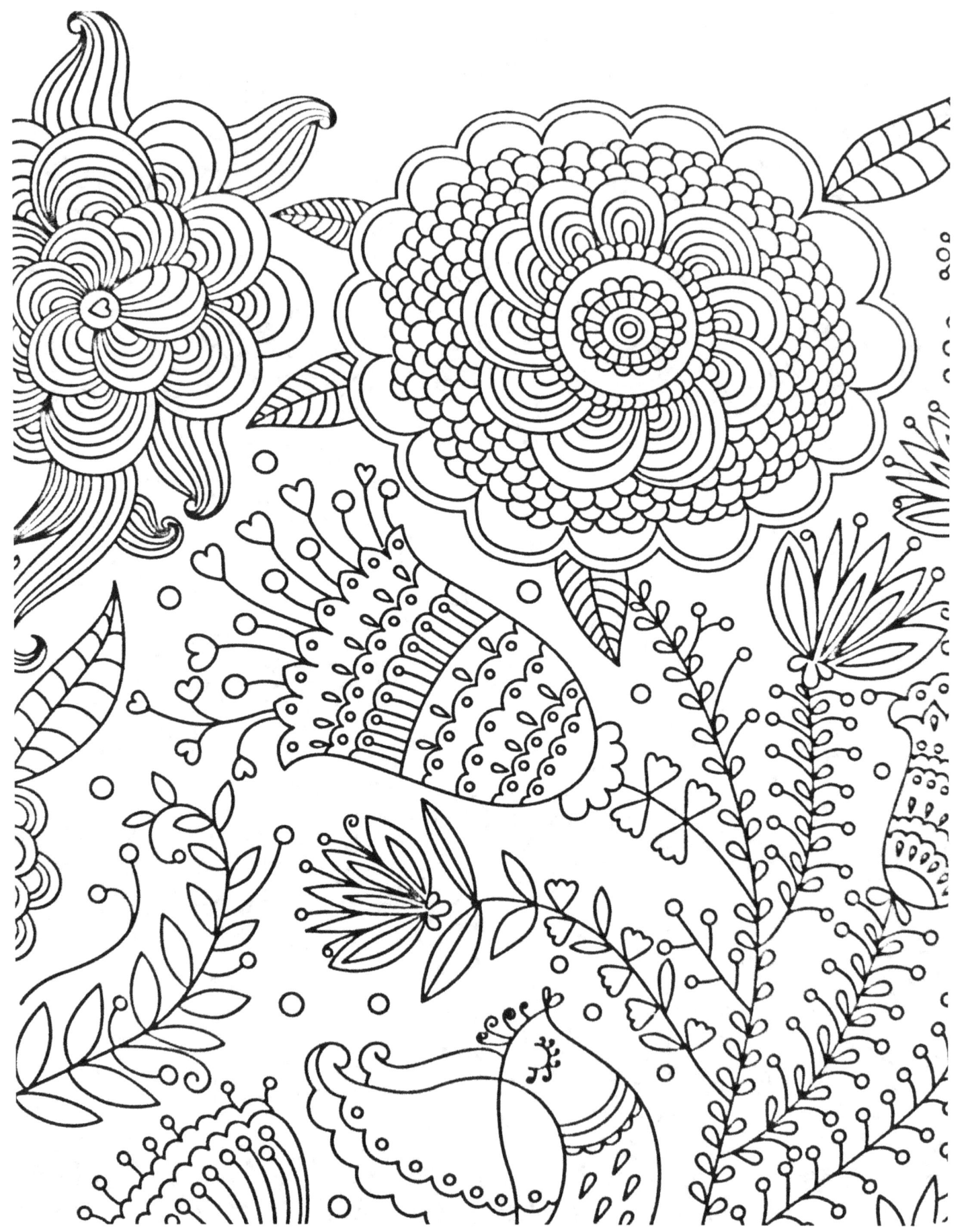

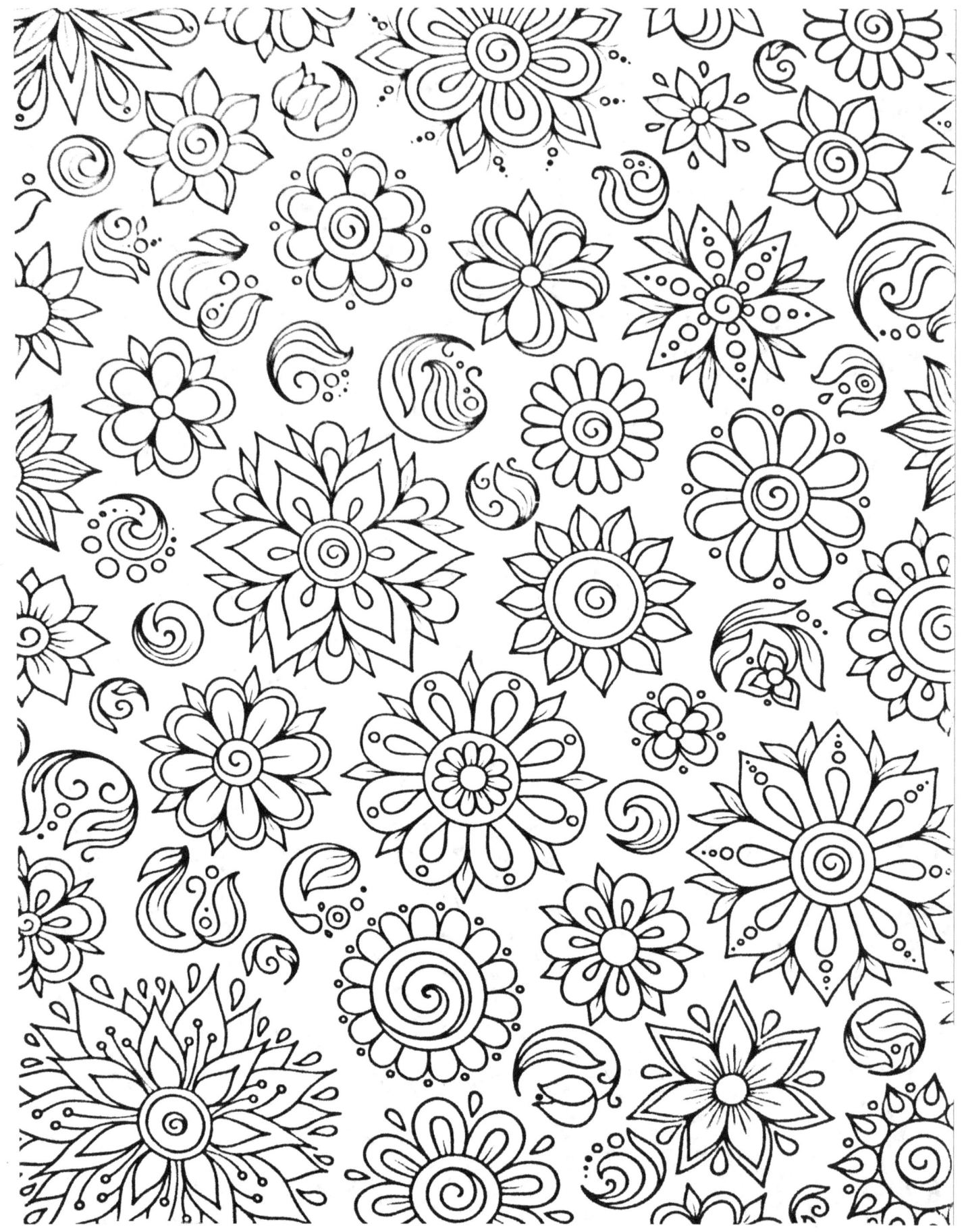

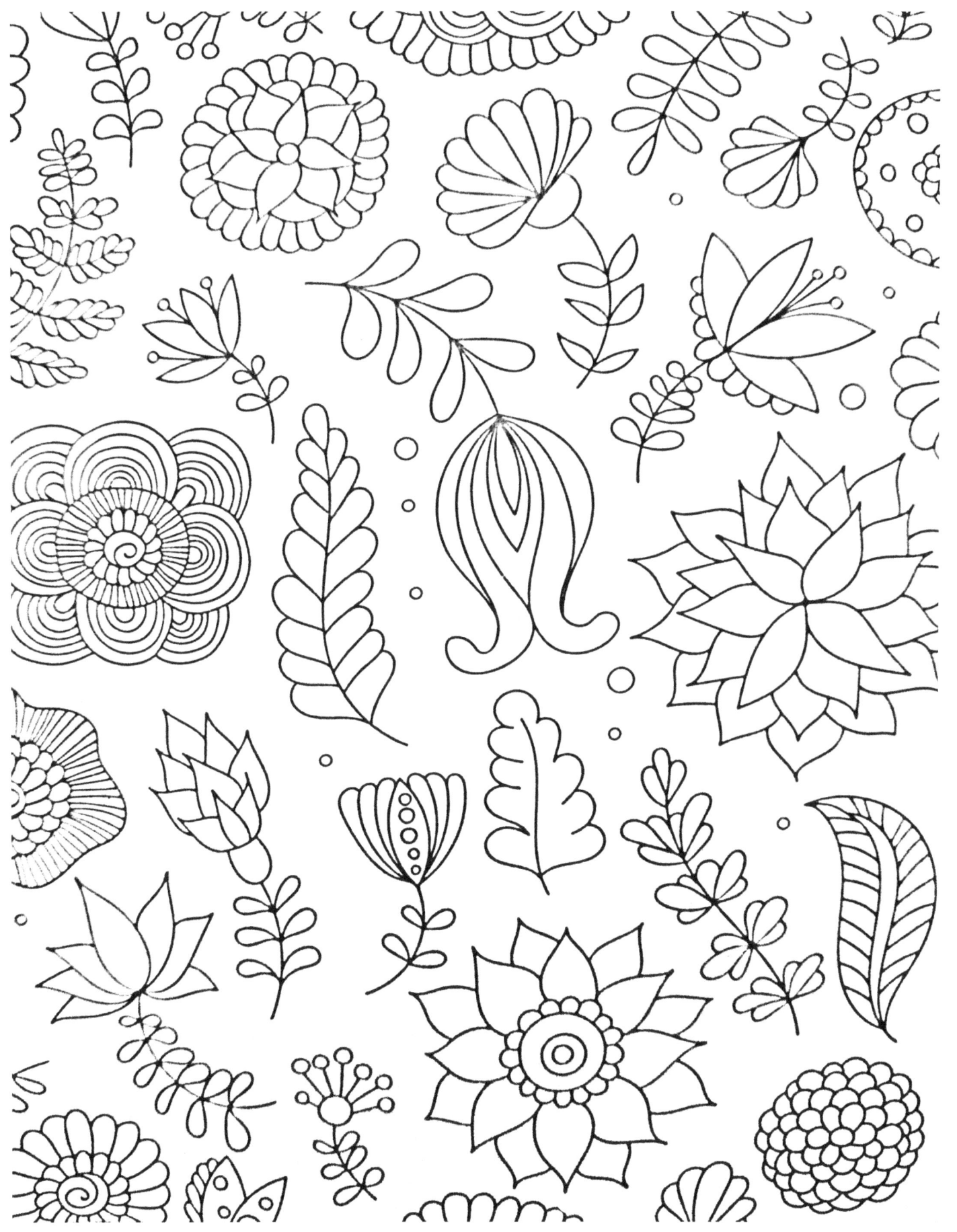

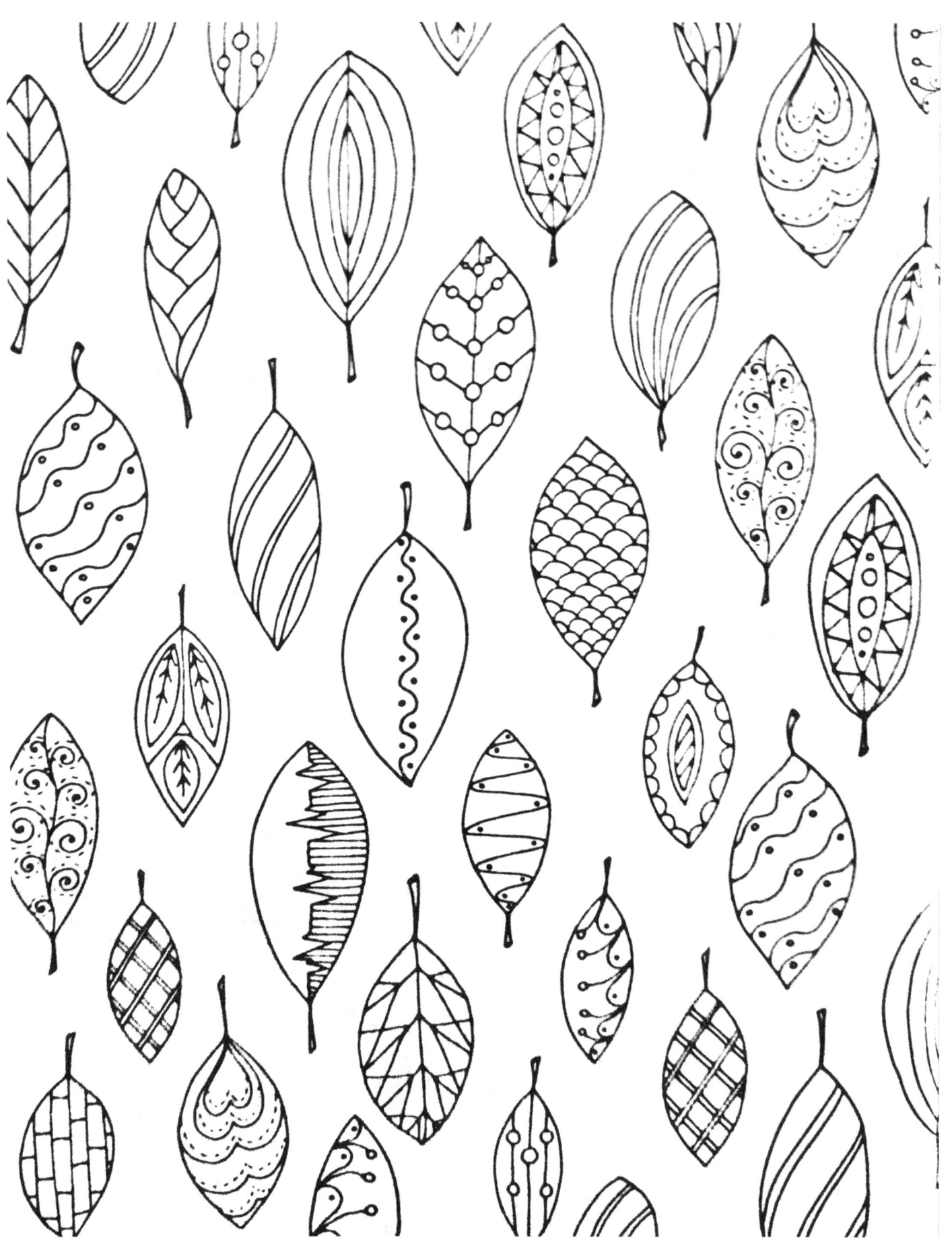

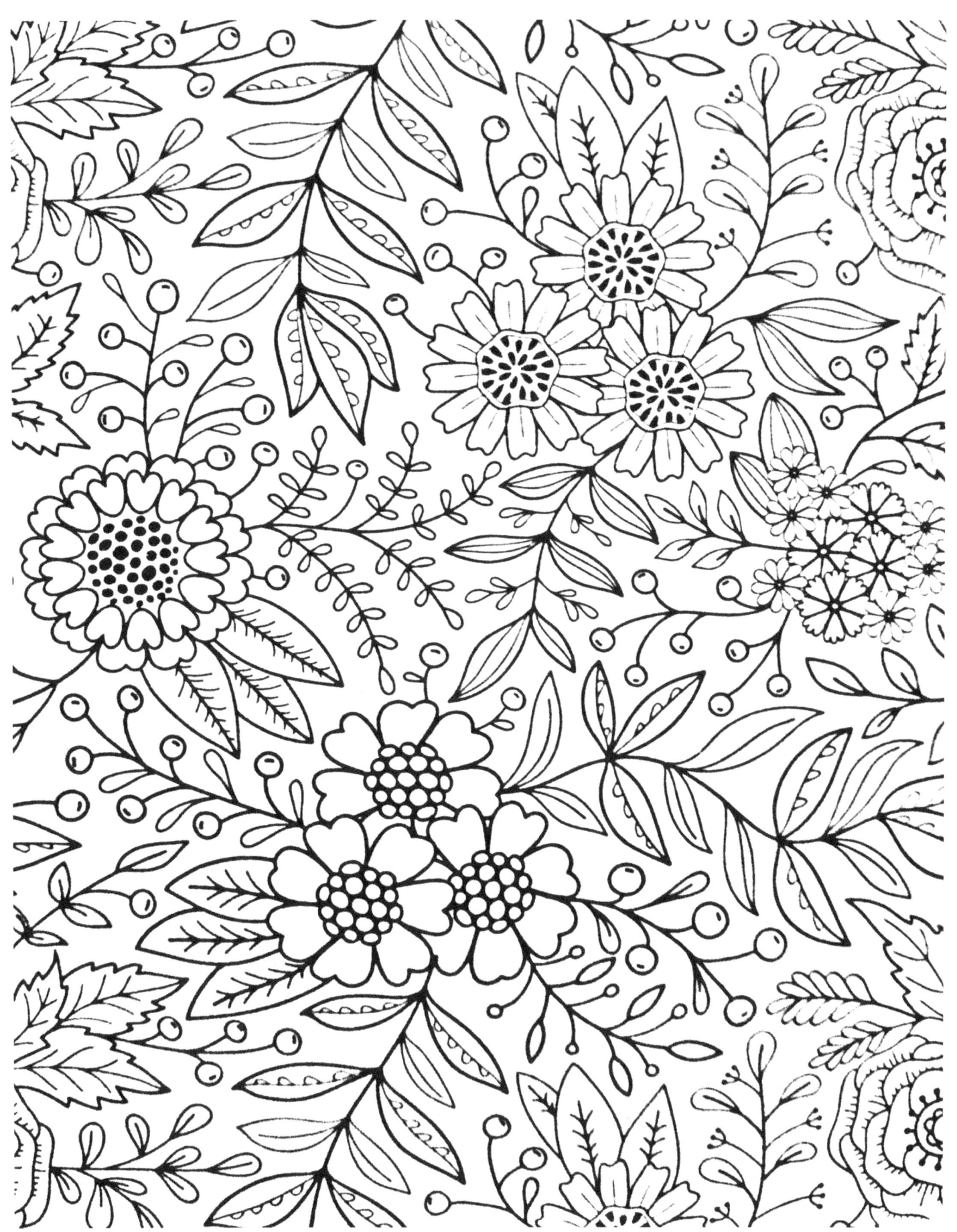

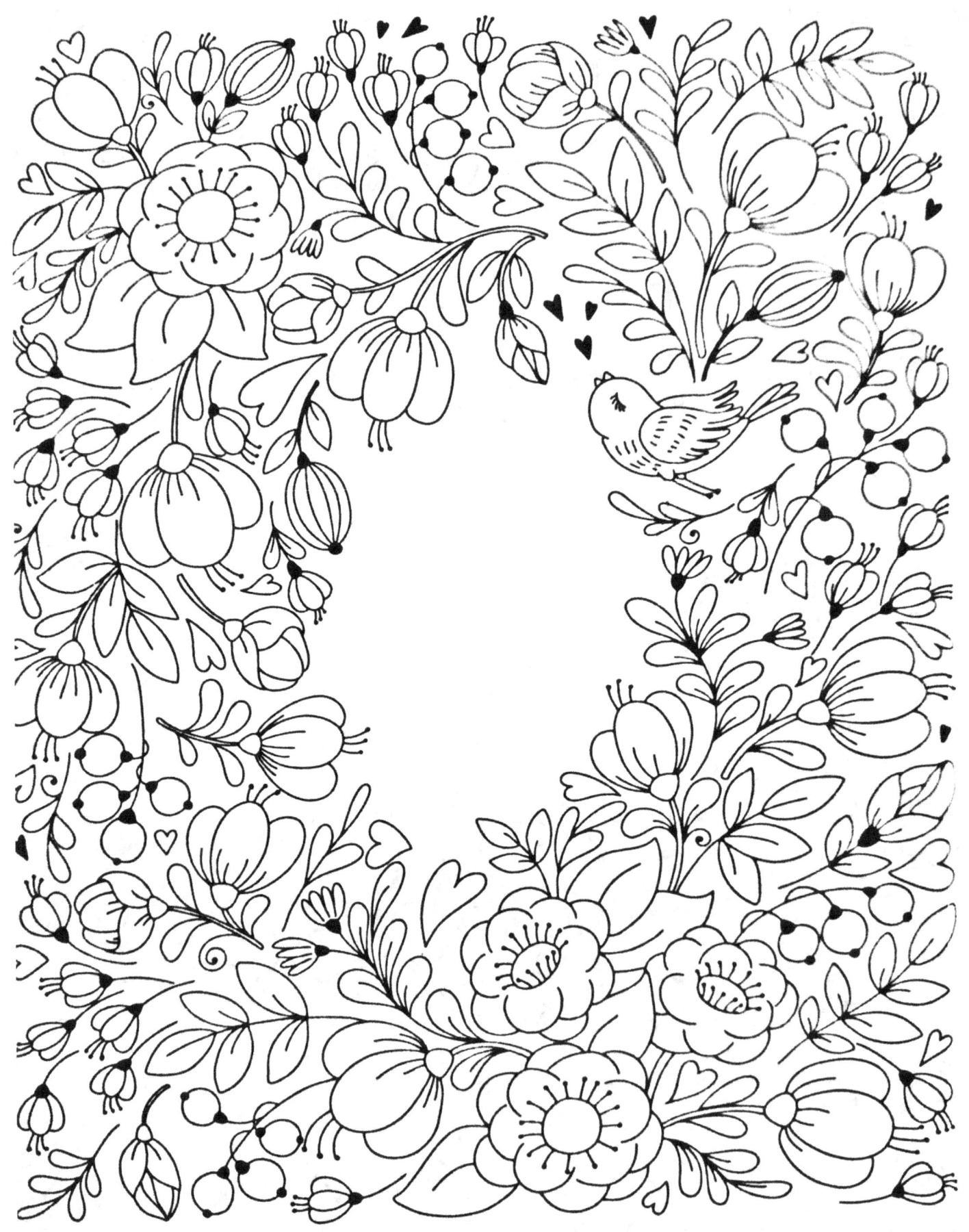

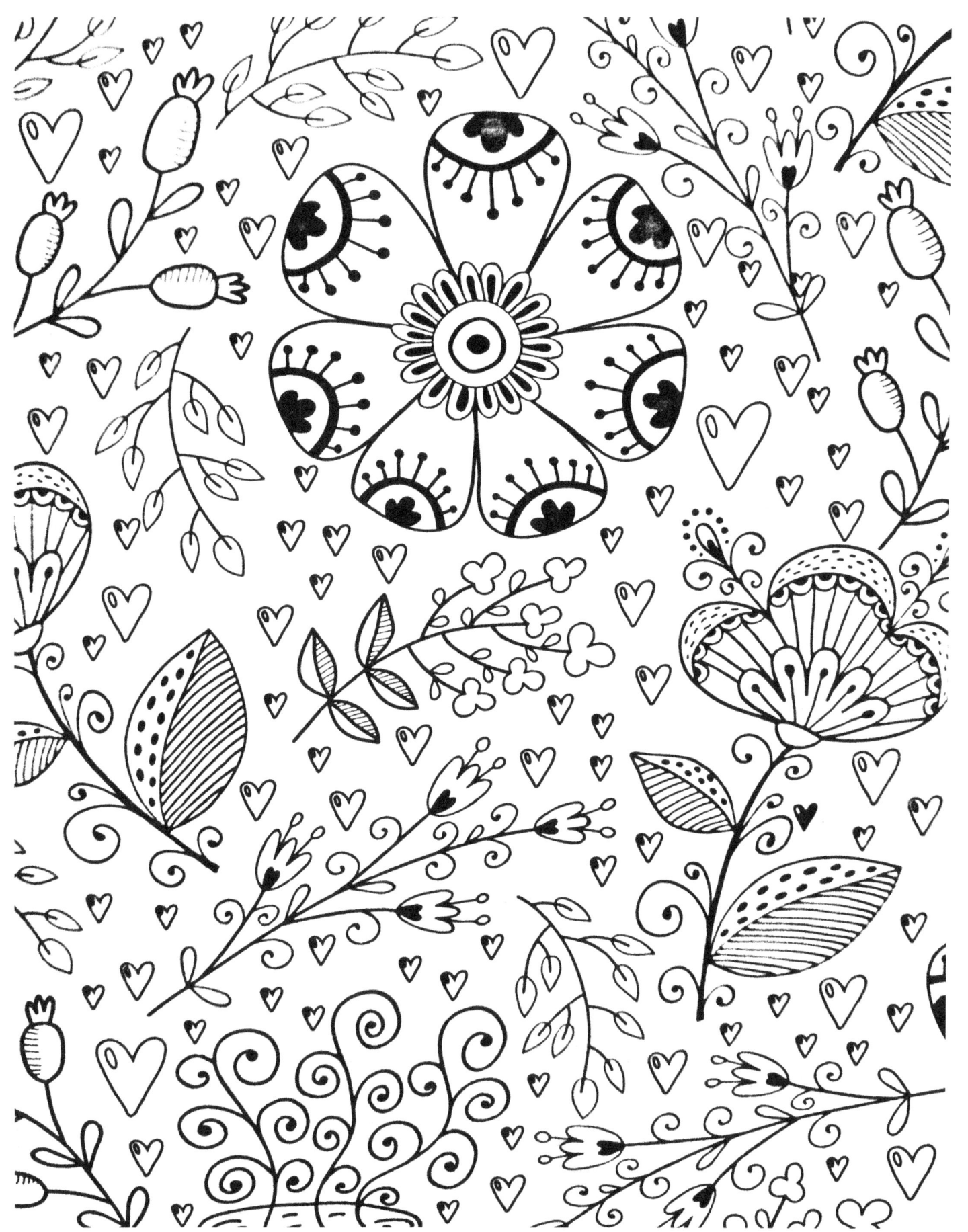

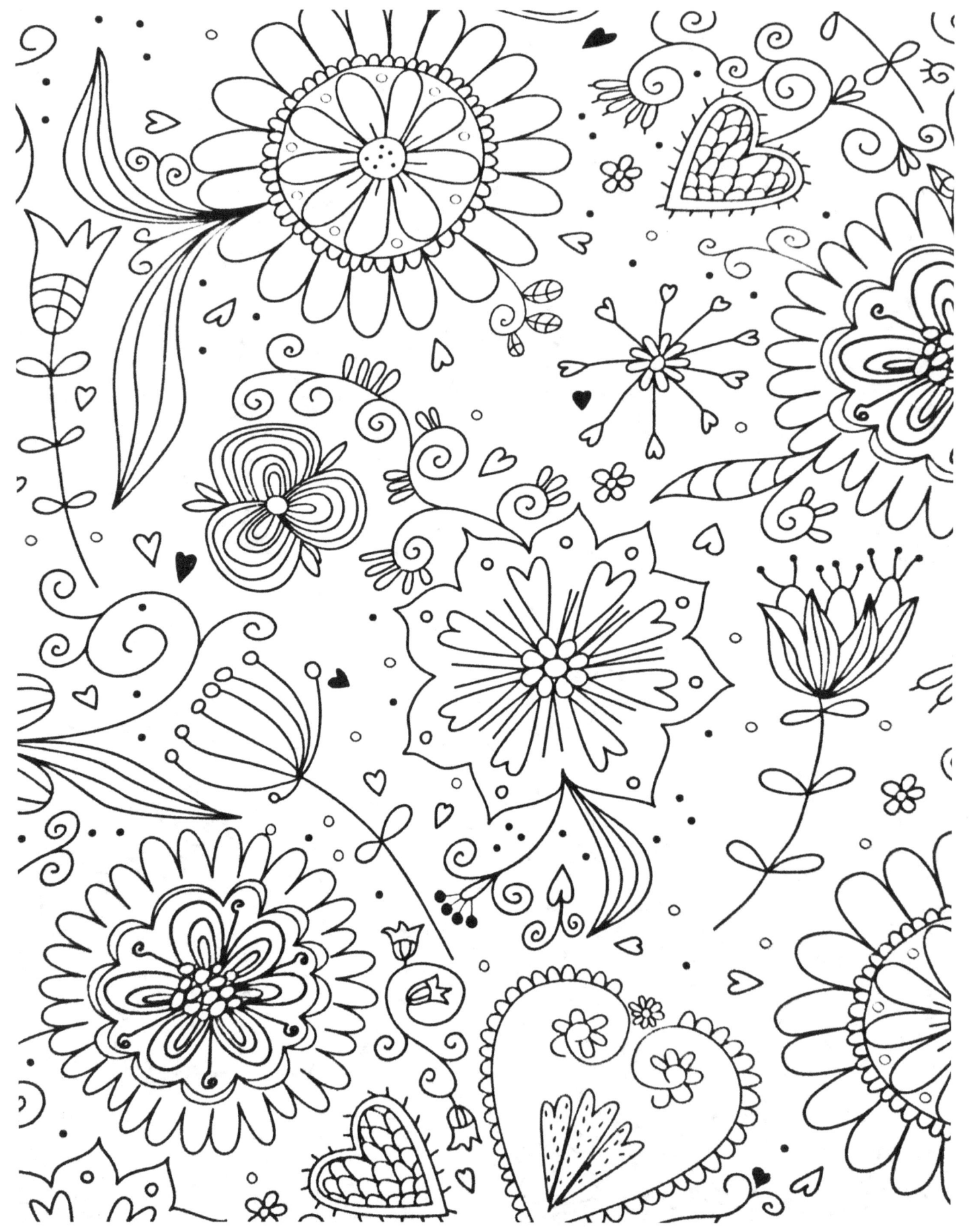

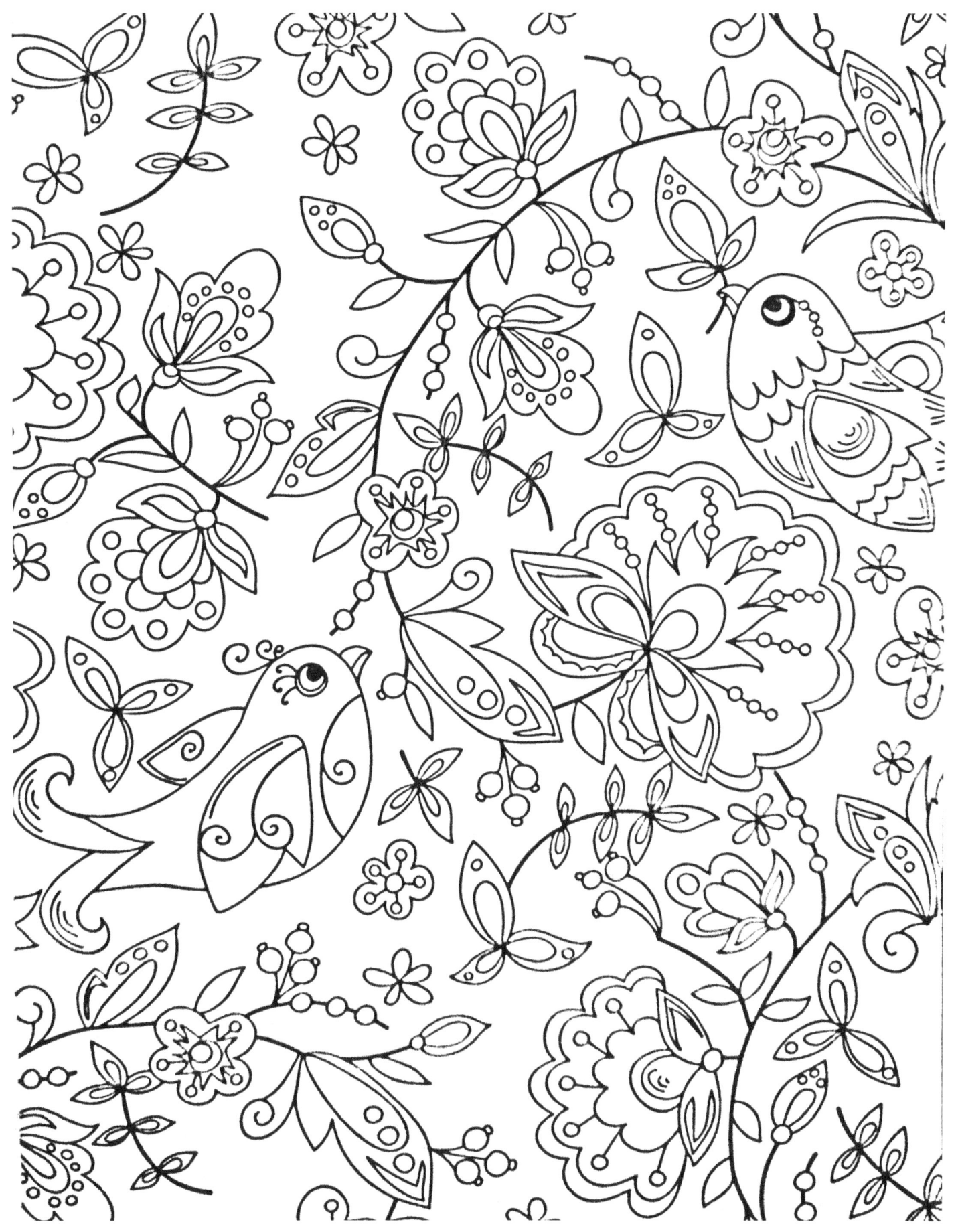

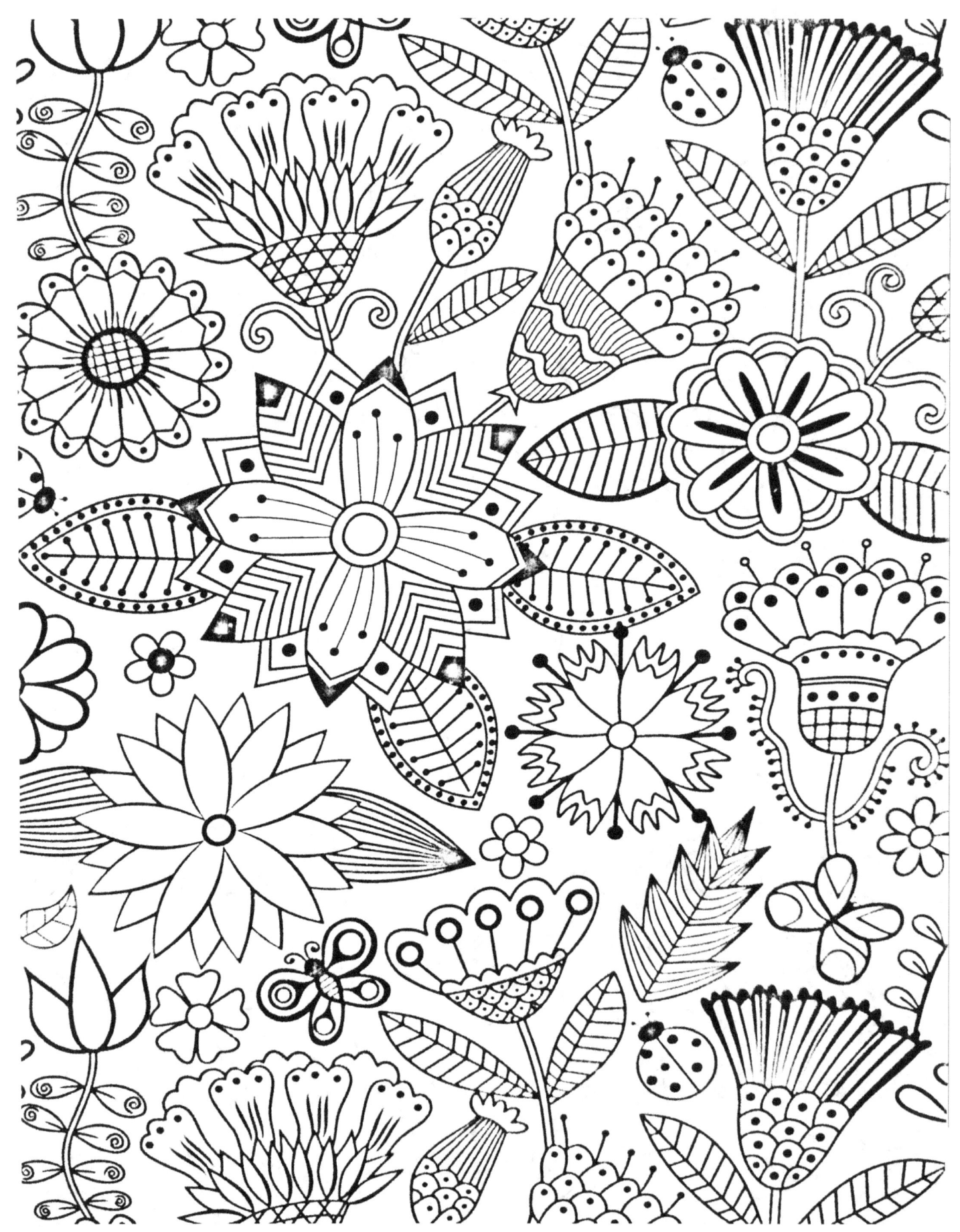

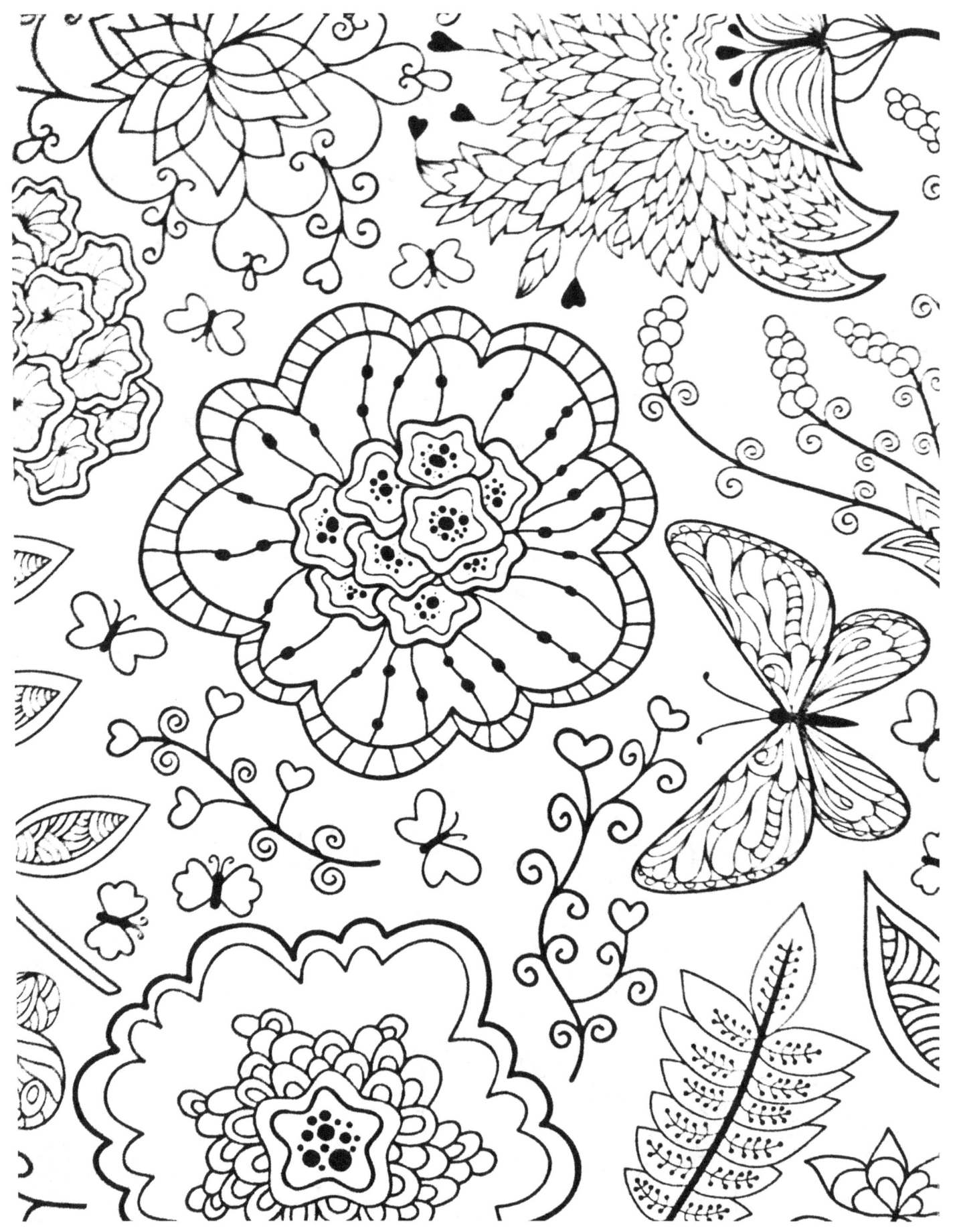

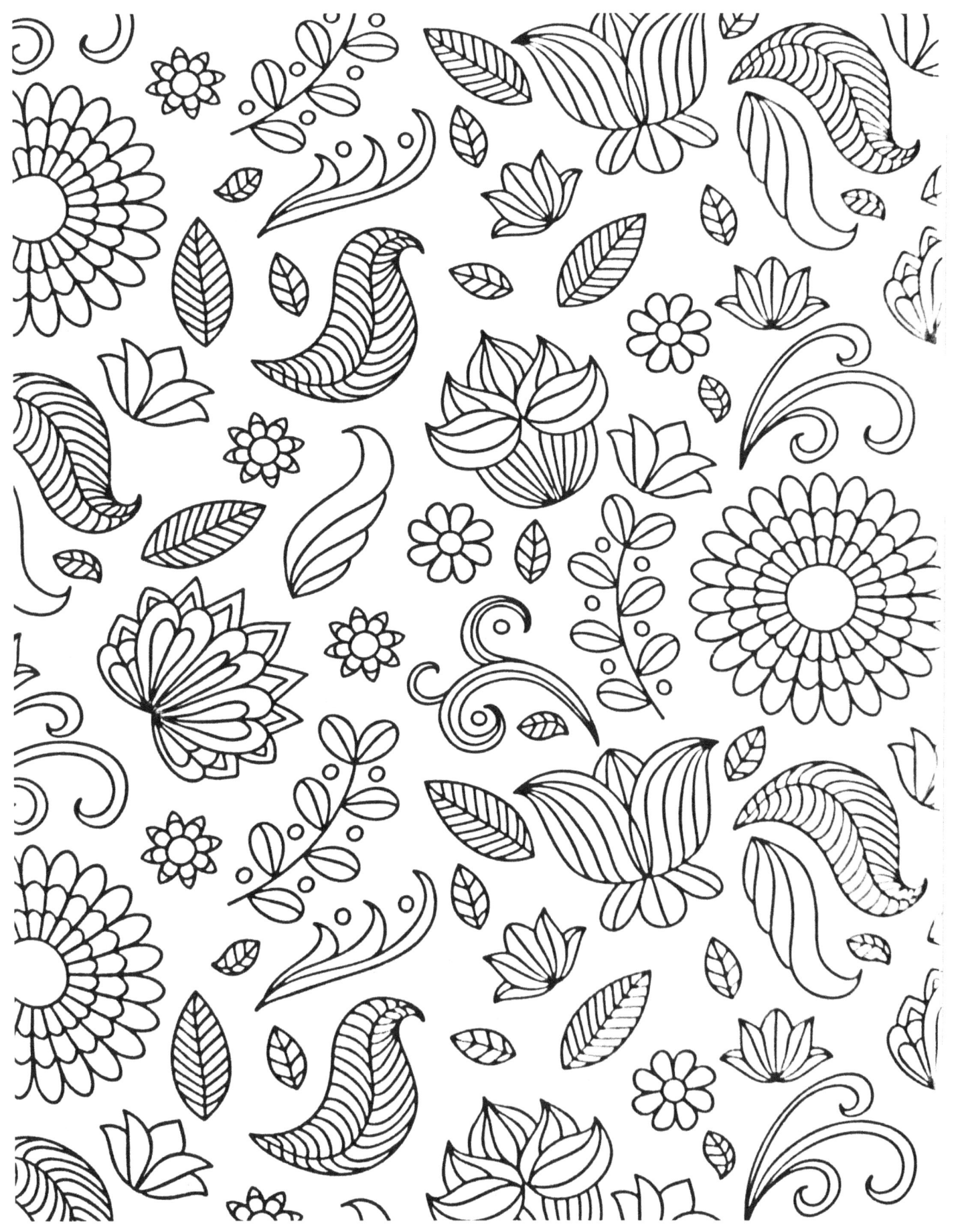

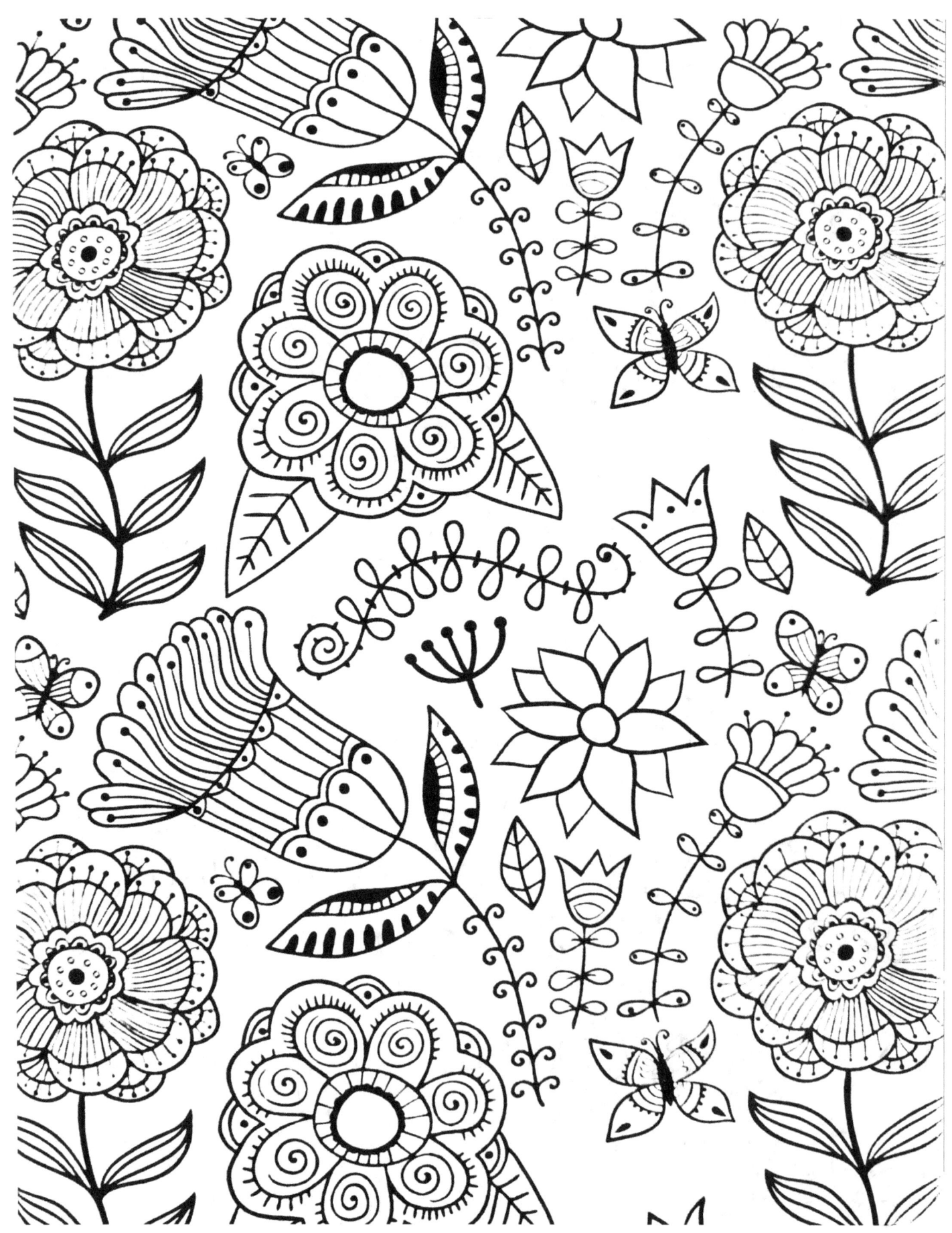

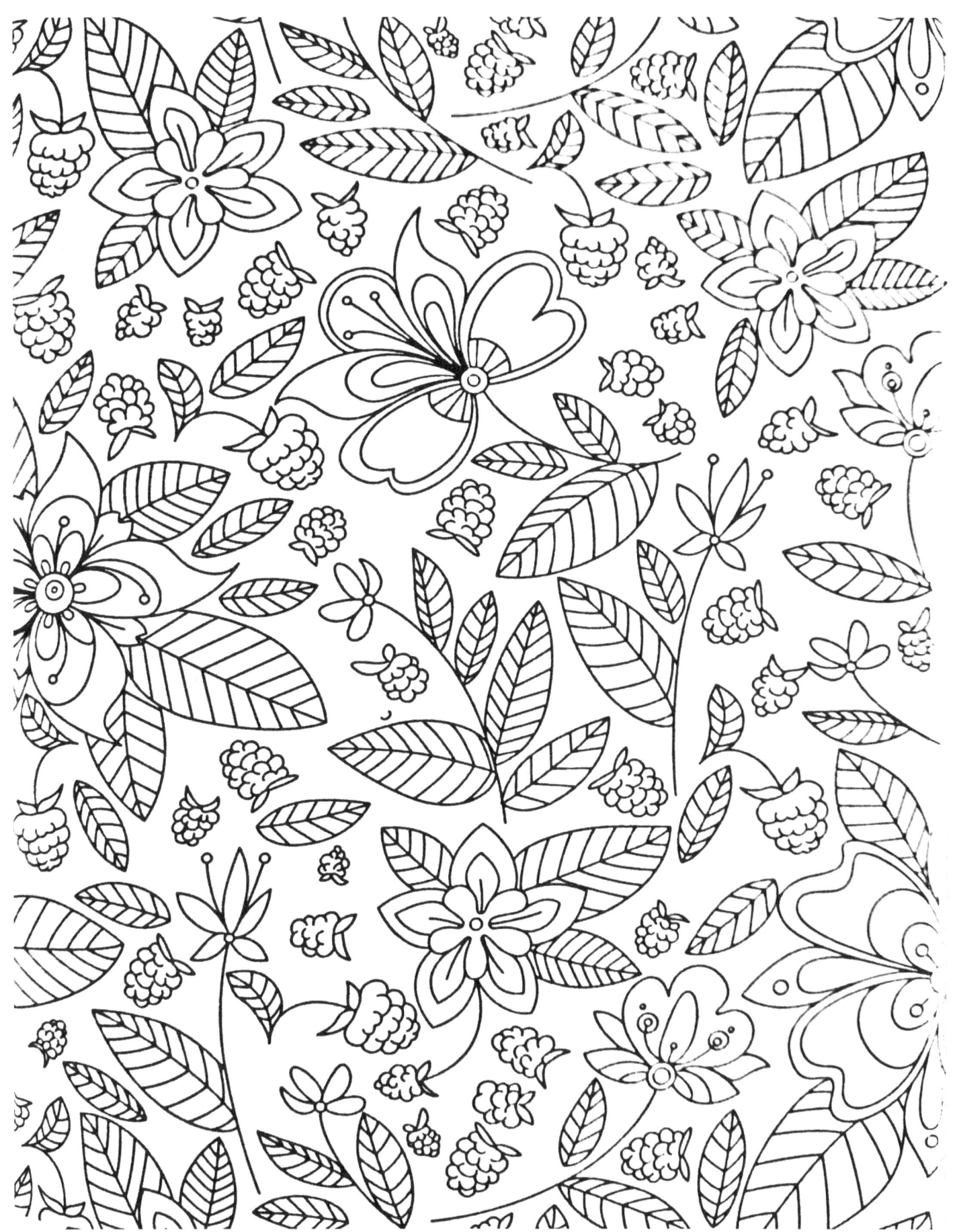

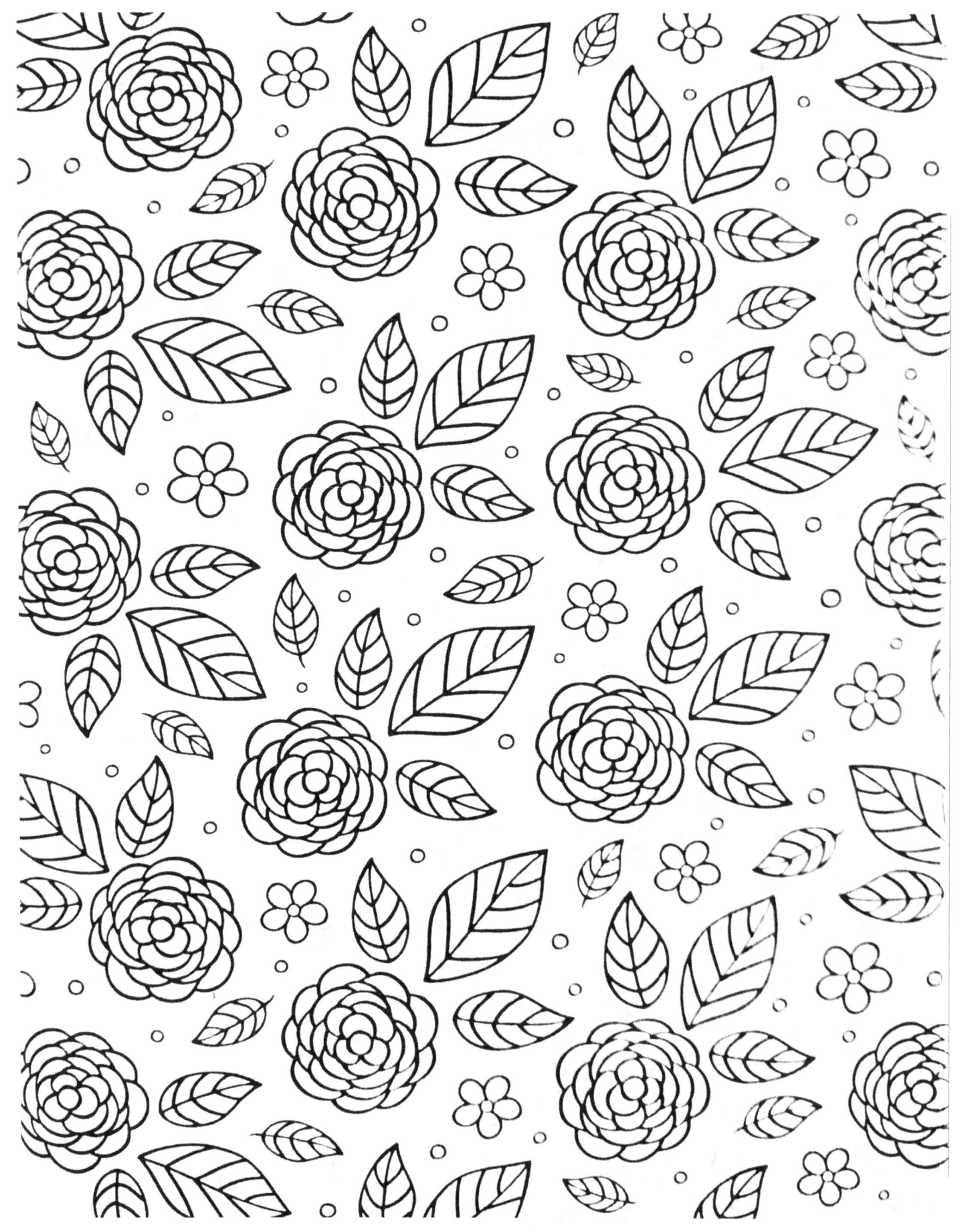

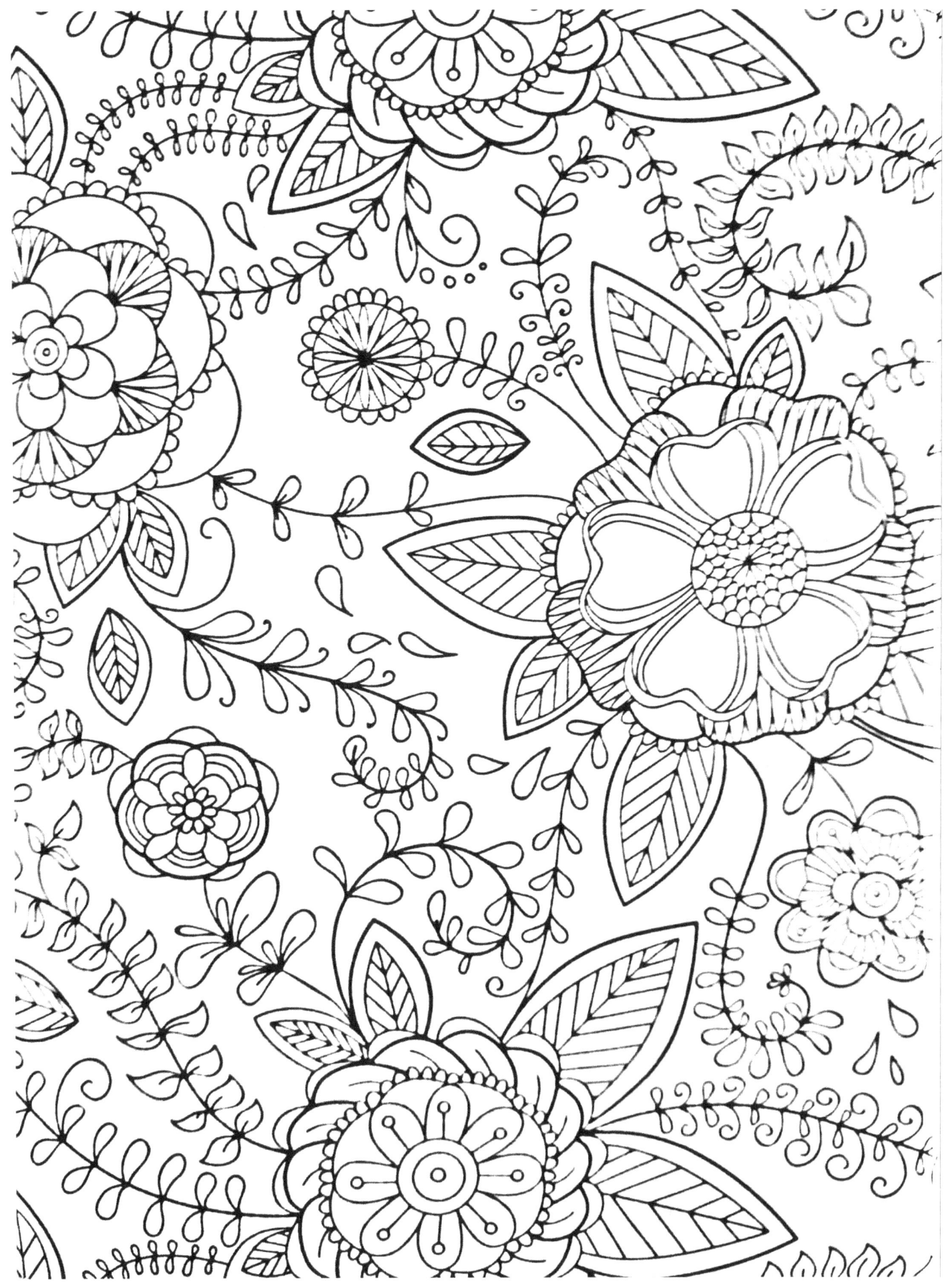

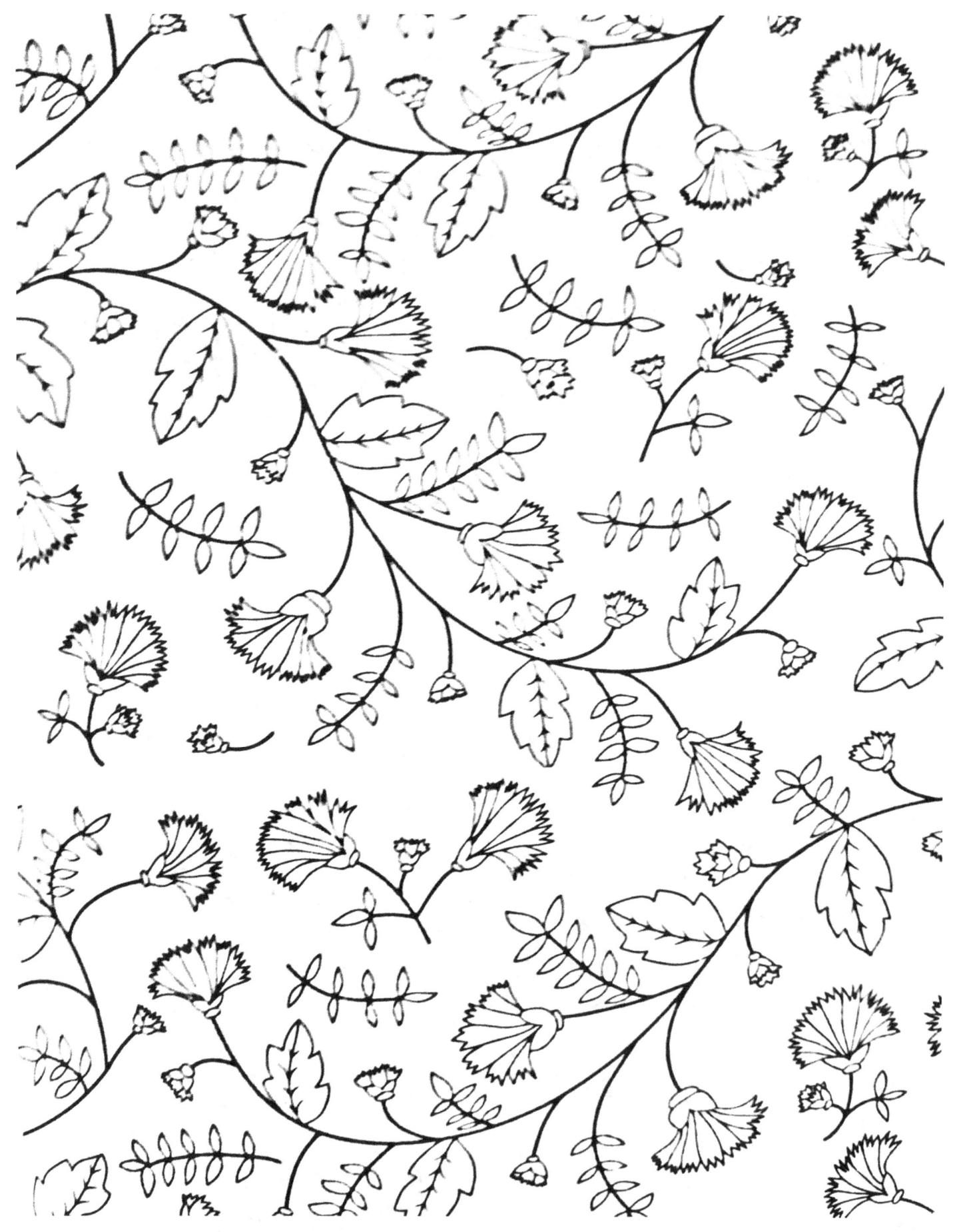

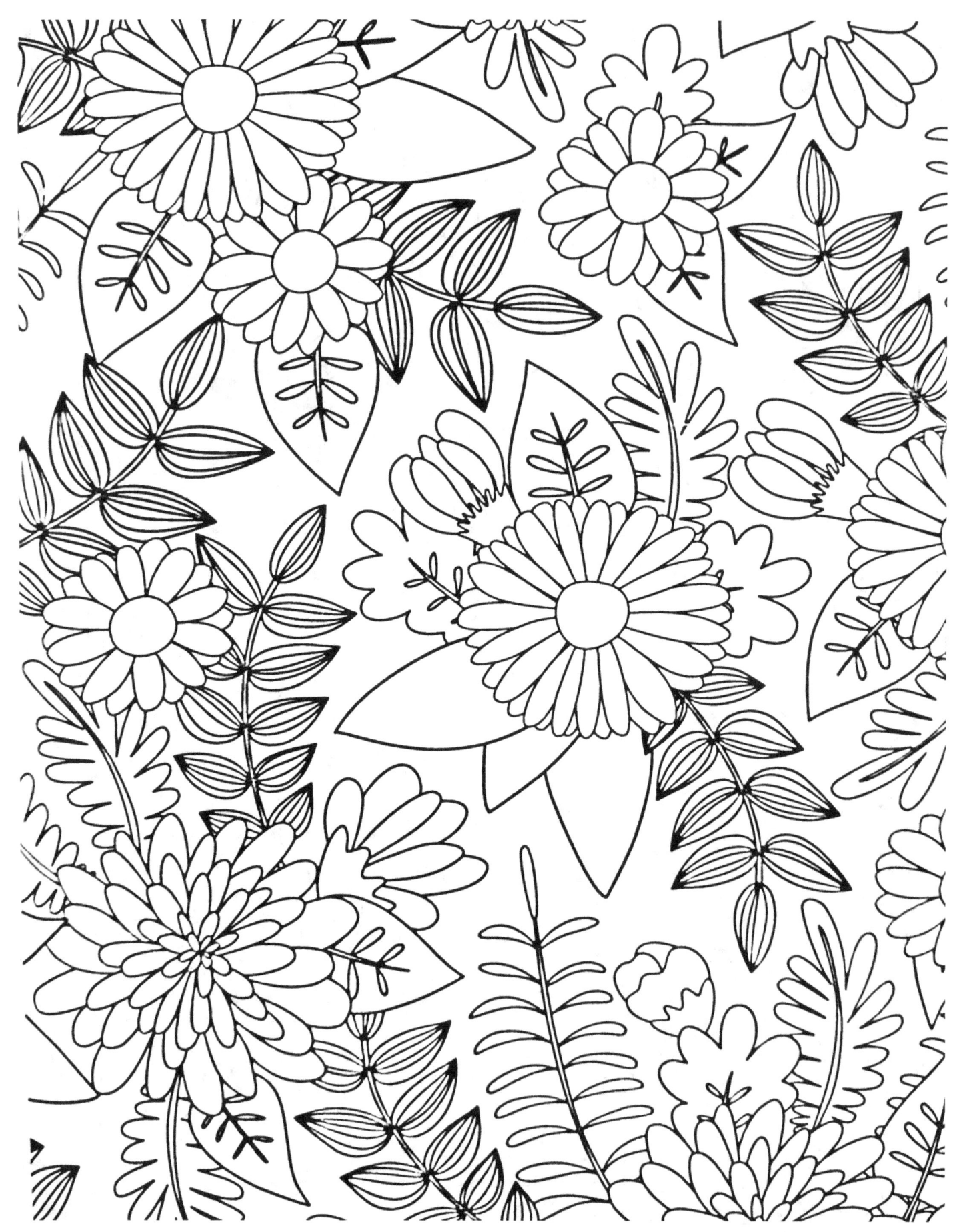

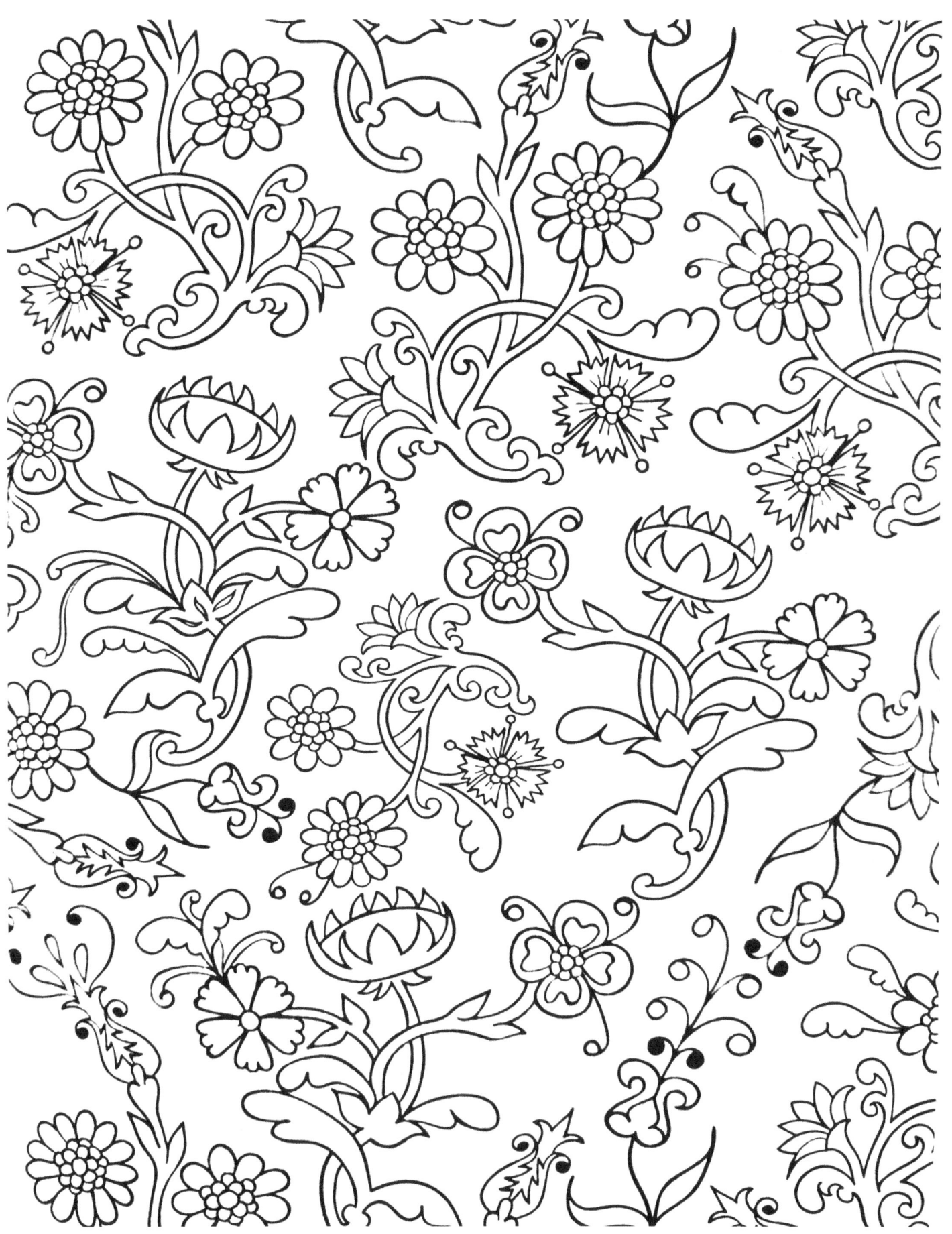

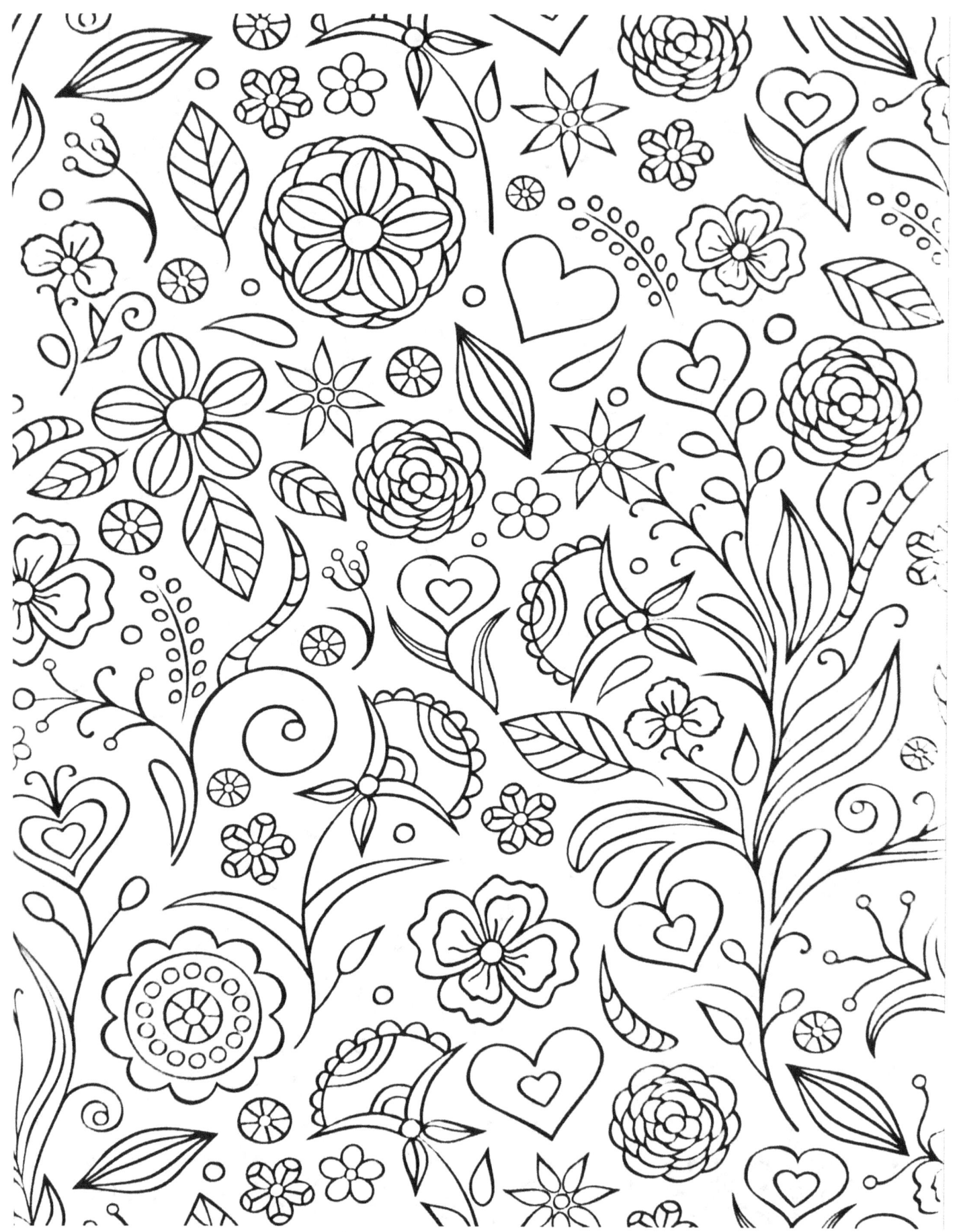

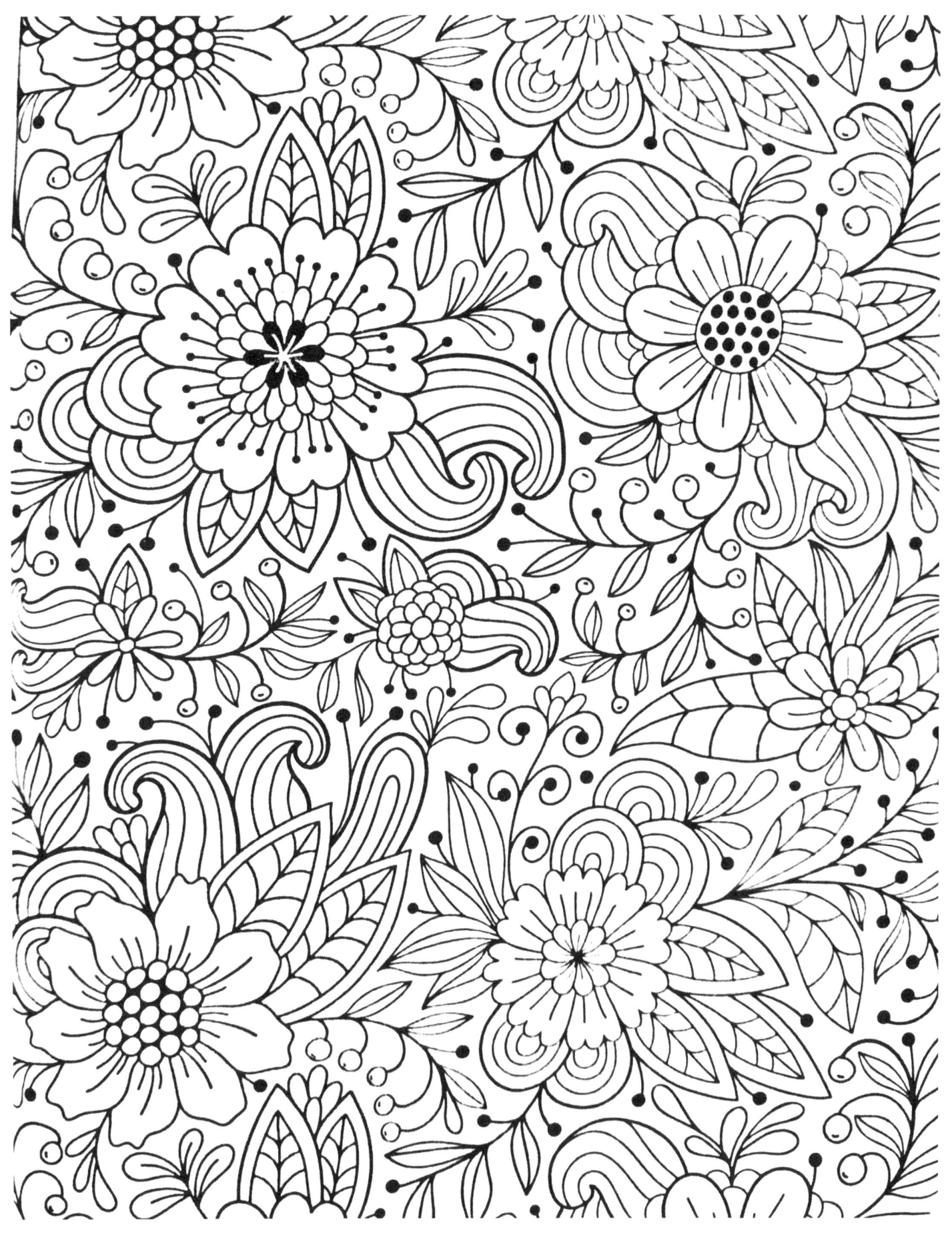

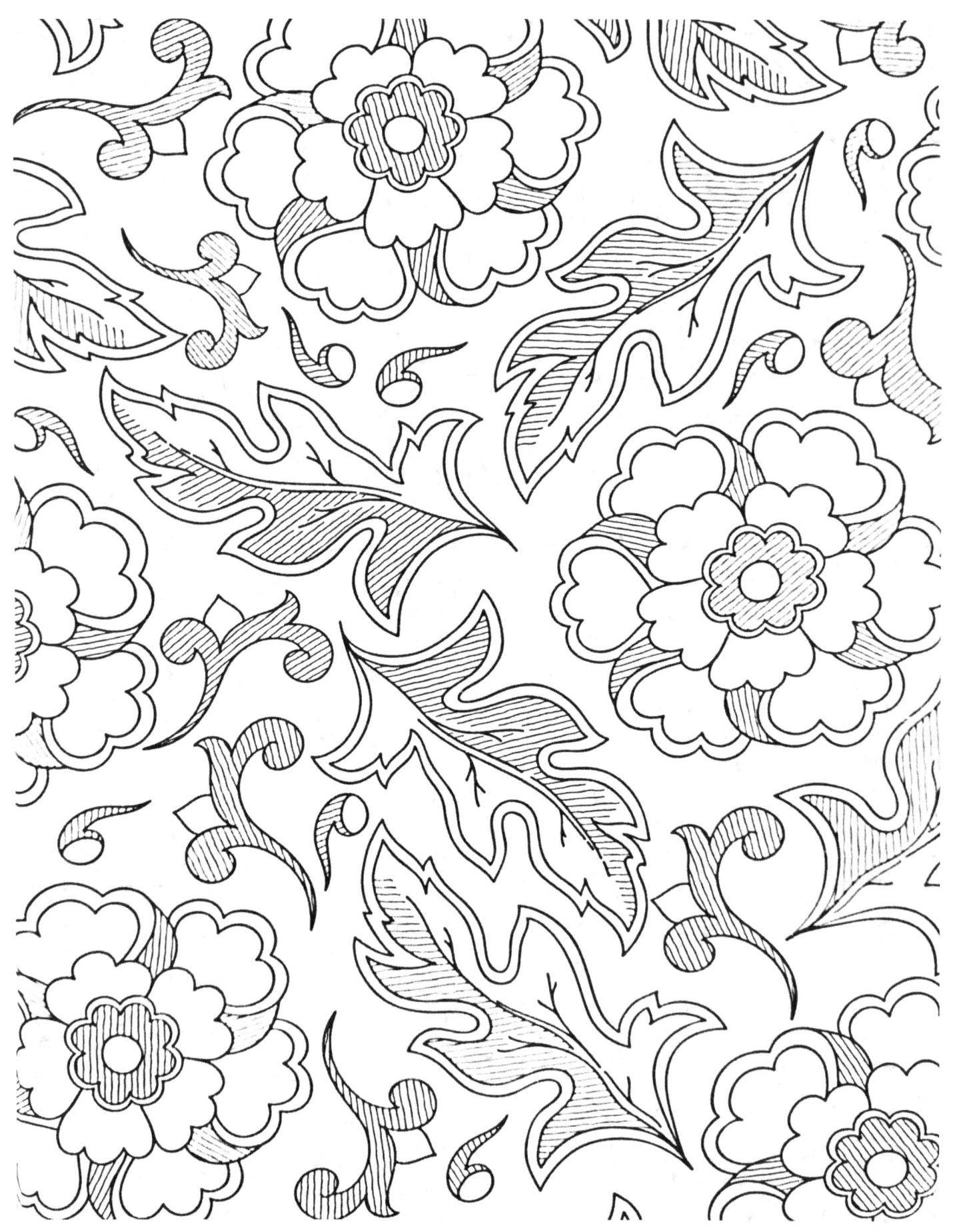

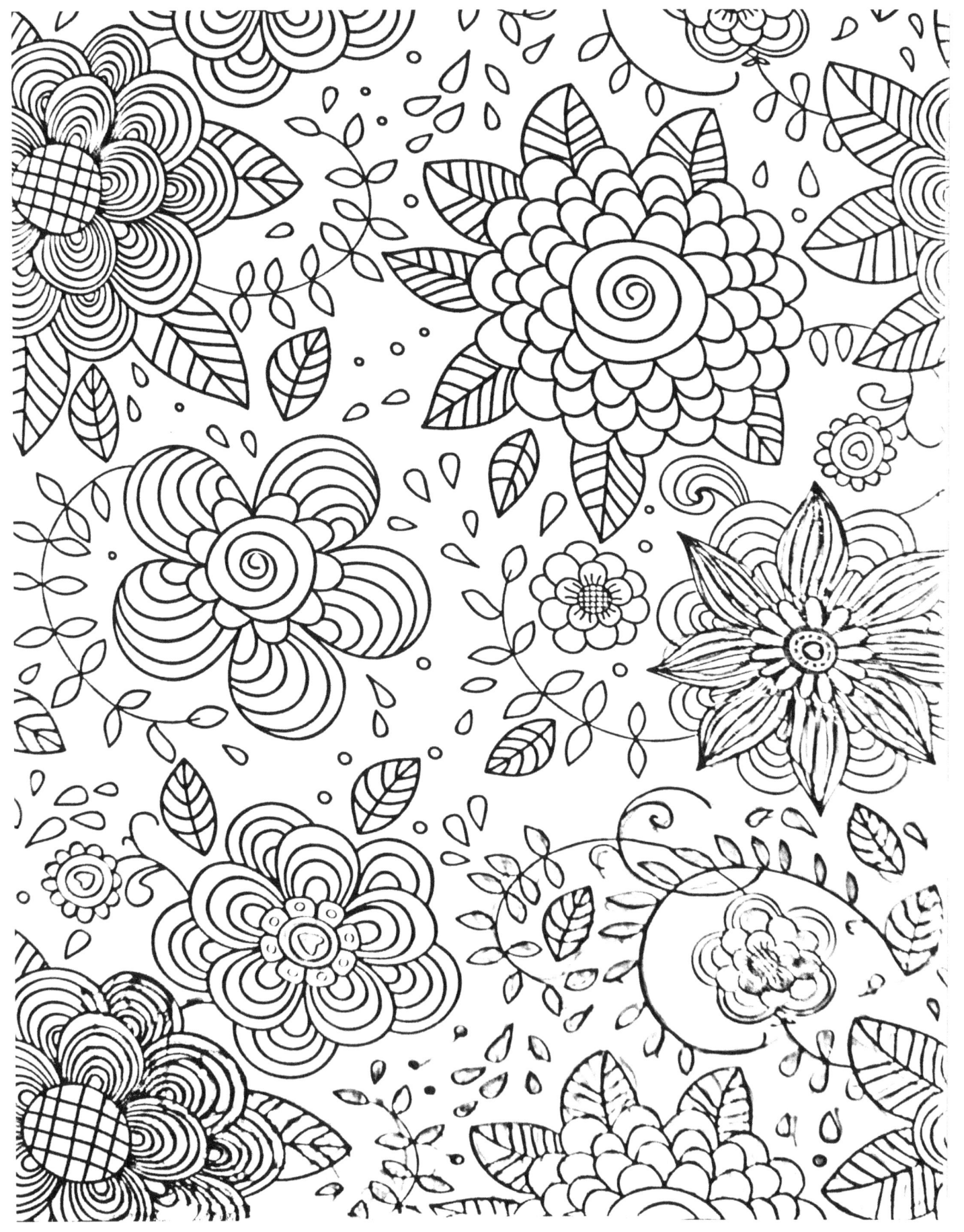

www.ingramcontent.com/pod-product-compliance
Lightning Source LLC
Chambersburg PA
CBHW081311180526
45170CB00007B/2657